‘Being in Ancient Egypt’ Thoughts on Agency, Materiality and Cognition

Proceedings of the seminar held in Copenhagen, September 29-30, 2006

Edited by

Rune Nyord
Annette Kjølby

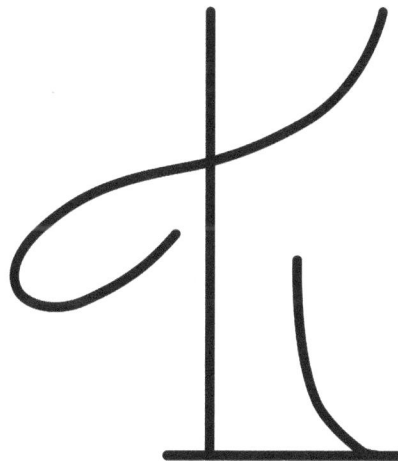

BAR International Series 2019
2009

Published in 2016 by
BAR Publishing, Oxford

BAR International Series 2019

'Being in Ancient Egypt'. Thoughts on Agency, Materiality and Cognition

ISBN 978 1 4073 0594 3

BAR Publishing is the trading name of British Archaeological Reports (Oxford) Ltd. British Archaeological Reports was first incorporated in 1974 to publish the BAR Series, International and British. In 1992 Hadrian Books Ltd became part of the BAR group. This volume was originally published by Archaeopress in conjunction with British Archaeological Reports (Oxford) Ltd / Hadrian Books Ltd, the Series principal publisher, in 2009. This present volume is published by BAR Publishing, 2016.

Printed in England

BAR
PUBLISHING

BAR titles are available from:

BAR Publishing
122 Banbury Rd, Oxford, OX2 7BP, UK
EMAIL info@barpublishing.com
PHONE +44 (0)1865 310431
FAX +44 (0)1865 316916
www.barpublishing.com

Contents

Preface

The papers presented in this volume are the results of a seminar held at the University of Copenhagen in September 2006. As implied by the title of the seminar, 'Being in Ancient Egypt - Thoughts on agency, materiality and cognition', we wanted to create a forum for presenting and discussing research on ancient Egypt dealing with questions of a more abstract or theoretical nature than those commonly posed in Egyptology and Egyptian archaeology.

The theme of the seminar was inspired by the recent theoretical advances in anthropology, archaeology and cognitive linguistics dealing with, *inter alia*, the topics of agency, materiality and cognition mentioned in the subtitle of the seminar.

In our view, such theoretical perspectives offer an important way to supplement more traditional empirical studies of ancient Egyptian sources, as well as raising a number of questions that - while they are not necessarily easily answered - provoke considerations of importance to our understanding of 'being in ancient Egypt'.

The seminar offered opportunities for discussing questions of perception and experience, choice and agency, and conceptions and consciousness from a number of different perspectives. Some of the papers presented here draw overtly on theoretical frameworks from outside the field of Egyptology, while others raise questions of a similar nature without explicit reference outside the field. A common feature for all the papers presented here is their attempt to open up new ways of approaching old questions or to pose completely new questions to well-known material.

In this volume, John Gee presents a new perspective on the old question of the constituents of the human being. Presenting a close examination of textual evidence relating to the notions of ka, ba and akh, Gee argues that on the basis of what the Egyptians themselves have to say about these concepts, they can be understood as "memory" or "fate" (ka); "soul" which also functions as a superordinate category of entities in the Egyptian cosmology (ba); and "angel" (akh), respectively.

Harold M. Hays revisits the well-known inscription of Icherneferet in the light of P. Bourdieu's sociological notion of *agency*, a theoretical expression of an individual's choices and actions within societal structures. A central question of agency in Egyptian autobiographical inscriptions is the role of the private individual in relation to the king, and the fact that Icherneferet's services for the king are of a ritual nature raises further questions of the delegation and displacement of agency.

Annette Kjølby discusses 'material agency' and object-human interaction involved in the creation, use and presence of New Kingdom private temple statues. The paper offers a theoretical discussion of attributed and experienced agency, material influence, and the object world as part of the extended or distributed person, mind and agency of human beings. It is considered how private statues contributed to the distributed personhood and extended presence of the individual represented. Furthermore, A. Gell's 'art nexus' has been used as an inspiration for examining various Agent/Patient relationships involving the statues.

Maya Müller explores the methodological possibilities of interpreting sculptural portraits of Senwosret III. The first part of the study consists of an examination of genetically and biologically determined features of the face as found in the portraits. On this basis, Müller moves on to study the personal expressions of the face, and it is argued that important insights can be gained by comparing the portraits of the king with those of well-known modern people showing similar expressions, thus offering a new way to approach interpretations of sculpture.

Rune Nyord proposes a method for combining the insights of philosophical phenomenology with traditional philological work. It is argued that our understanding of Egyptian terminology of body parts and the expressions in which they occur can be improved by adopting the phenomenological conceptual apparatus of the philosopher H. Schmitz, which makes it possible, *inter alia*, to avoid the traditional Western mind-body dualism and to achieve a much more nuanced understanding of particular Egyptian expressions. As example of the usability of the method, the Egyptian term *ḥ3ty*, "heart" is studied from a phenomenological perspective.

John Tait presents a study of the conceptualization and use of anger, primarily in Demotic literary texts. In these texts, anger often occurs in particular fixed key phrases, more often than not as openly demonstrative outbursts that serve, from the point of view of narrative structure, to advance the storyline. Another characteristic feature of anger is the fact that displays of anger are mainly a royal and divine prerogative.

David A. Warburton challenges the conventional view that artifacts are to be interpreted in verbal terms, suggesting that Egyptian art may well contain thoughts which are only later, if at all, put into linguistic form. On this basis, various previous approaches to Egyptian concepts of such categories as time, space and color are discussed, leading to a suggestion of how Egyptian art can be used as a source for gaining insight into such abstract notions.

We are grateful to the Institute of Cross-Cultural and Regional Studies at the University of Copenhagen for providing a venue for the seminar and to cand. mag. Mette Gregersen for kindly helping us with a number of practical details.

Rune Nyord and Annette Kjølby
Copenhagen, August 2009

A New Look at the Conception of the Human Being in Ancient Egypt

John Gee

In a book designed to show the similarities between ancient Egyptian religion and religious ideas of modern African tribes, E. A. W. Budge divided the conception of the human being into different 'portion[s] of a man's entity.'[1] He listed them as the body (*ẖ.t*),[2] the *k3* or 'double,'[3] the *sʿḥ* or 'spirit-body,'[4] the *šw.t* or 'shadow,'[5] the *b3* or 'body-soul,'[6] the *ib* or 'heart,'[7] and the *3ẖ* or 'spirit-soul'[8]. I have updated Budge's transliteration, which he knew was misleading and out-of-date,[9] but retained his translations. In terms of Egyptology, Budge seems very much ancient history, but the concept of dividing the human being into parts is still with us. A recent work divides what is termed 'human nature' into the *ḥʿ* 'the body,' the *šwt* 'the shadow,' the *b3*, the *k3* the 'life force' or 'double,' and the *rn* 'the name.'[10] Though the details have changed, the overall picture is still similar:

1911 (Budge)	2000 (Allen)
ẖ.t 'body'	*ḥʿ* 'body'
k3 'double'	*k3* 'life-force or double'
sʿḥ 'spirit-body'	
šw.t 'shadow'	*šw.t* 'shadow'
b3 'body-soul'	*b3*
ib 'heart'	
3ẖ 'spirit-soul'	
	rn 'name'

Not everyone has been satisfied with the proposed divisions of the human being. Žabkar claimed that 'the Ba was never considered to be one of the constituent parts of a human composite.'[11] Instead, he claimed that the *b3* 'was considered to represent the man himself, the totality of his physical and psychic capacities.'[12] But Žabkar's view on this point has been largely ignored in favor of a division of the human being.[13]

---

1 Budge, E.A.W., *Osiris and the Egyptian Resurrection*, London 1911, reprint New York, 1973, p. 2:117.
2 Budge, *Osiris and the Egyptian Resurrection*, p. 2:117.
3 Budge, *Osiris and the Egyptian Resurrection*, pp. 2:117-23.
4 Budge, *Osiris and the Egyptian Resurrection*, pp. 2:123-25.
5 Budge, *Osiris and the Egyptian Resurrection*, pp. 2:126-128.
6 Budge, *Osiris and the Egyptian Resurrection*, pp. 2:128-30.
7 Budge, *Osiris and the Egyptian Resurrection*, pp. 2:130-32.
8 Budge, *Osiris and the Egyptian Resurrection*, pp. 2:132-35.
9 See the remarks in Budge, E.A.W., *An Egyptian Hieroglyphic Dictionary*, London 1920, pp. 1:lix-lxii
10 Allen, J.P., *Middle Egyptian. An Introduction to the Language and Culture of Hieroglyphs*, Cambridge 2000, pp. 79-81.
11 Žabkar, L.V., *A Study of the Ba Concept in Ancient Egyptian Texts* (=*SAOC* 34), Chicago 1968, p. 3.
12 Žabkar, *A Study of the Ba Concept in Ancient Egyptian Texts*, p. 3.
13 Perhaps exceptional is Ward, W.A., *The Four Egyptian Homographic Roots B-3*, Rome 1978, p. 69.

The first thing to notice about the various lists of parts of the human being is that they do not derive directly from Egyptian texts. There are texts that list the parts of the human body,[14] but are there Egyptian texts that list the parts of the human being? Gardiner and others have thought to have found in the tomb of Amenemhet just such a text,[15] actually a pair of texts.[16] Both texts are unusual formulas accompanying offering scenes whose beginning is missing, the first stating that the offerings are:

n kꜣ=f	for his ka
n ꜥbꜣ=f n ipn imy ẖr.t-nṯr	for this offering stone of his that is in the god's domain
n šꜣy	for (his) fate
n ꜥḥꜥ=f	for his lifetime
n msḫ.t=f	for his birthplace
n rnn.t=f	for his good fortune
n ẖnm=f	for his dependents

The second list is as follows:

n kꜣ=f	for his ka
n ꜥbꜣ=f [. . .]	for his offering stone [. . .]
[. . .]	[. . .]
n ꜣḫ=f	for his akh
n ẖꜣ.t=f	for his body
n šw.t=f	for his shadow
n ḫprw=f nb	for all his forms[17]

Both lists begin identically and then diverge. The first list seems to be a description of extrinsic characteristics about a human being: his fate, his lifetime, his good fortune, his dependents. The second list contains those things Egyptologists have typically associated with the parts of a human being, those that are intrinsic to a human being: his ka, his akh, his body, his shadow, his forms, and (according to Sethe's restoration of the lacuna) his ba.[18] But the most interesting thing about both of these lists is the inclusion of an offering stone at the beginning, which leads one to suspect that this is not simply a list of parts of the human being, since an offering stone is neither an intrinsic nor an extrinsic part of a human being. The separation of the ka from the rest of the list by the offering stone and the repetition in both makes one wonder whether the ka should be included as a part of either list. The inclusion of the ba, as a restoration in a unique passage, cannot be certain. Still, the list of the intrinsic parts of a human being serves as a starting point for our discussion.

In this paper, I will put forth an alternative to the standard understanding of the parts of the human being. I will analyze them from a particular methodological standpoint, and look at the ways the various parts are understood and interact. Because the list is lengthy, I will concentrate on three facets: the ba, the ka, and the akh.

---

[14] E.g. BD 42; the Metternich Stele (MMA 50.85), front, lines 9-35, in Allen, J.P., *The Art of Medicine in Ancient Egypt*, New York 2005, p. 54, and Sander-Hansen, C.E., *Die Texte der Metternichstele* (=*Analecta Aegyptiaca* 7), København 1956, pp. 20-27; MMA 35.9.21 19/10-20/11, in Goyon, J.-C., *Le Papyrus d'Imouthès Fils de Psintaês Au Metropolitan Museum of Art de New-York (Papyrus MMA 35.9.21)*, New York 1999, pls. XIX-XXA.

[15] Davies, N.d.G., and Gardiner, A. H., *The Tomb of Amenemhēt (No. 82)*, London 1915, pp. 98-100; Quaegebeur, J., *Le dieu égyptien Shaï dans la religion et l'onomastique* (=*OLA* 2), Leuven 1975, pp. 133-34.

[16] *Urk.* IV 1060-61.

[17] Davies and Gardiner, *The Tomb of Amenemhēt*, pls. XIX-XX, XXII-XXIII; *Urk.* IV 1060-61.

[18] *Urk.* IV 1061.

Method

Our goal is to understand what the ancient Egyptians understood by and about certain concepts. Since we do not have living informants to correct us, the following points of method should be observed:

(1) Insider statements are more important and carry more weight than outsider statements. So, obviously, statements by ancient Egyptians about their own religion carry more weight than statements by ancient Greek or Roman authors about the ancient Egyptian religion or, less obviously, than statements by modern Egyptologists about the ancient Egyptian religion. The primary sources are of more importance than secondary or tertiary sources.

(2) We need to always remember that the ancient Egyptian religion had no theology. 'There was no explicit and coherent explanation of Egyptian theology on the metalevel of theoretical discourse in ancient Egypt any more than there were theoretical explications in other areas, such as grammar, rhetoric, or historiography.'[19] Assmann reminds us that 'we can certainly think of religions that get along without explicit theology.'[20] Ancient Egyptian is one of these but by no means the only one. For example, in Eastern Orthodox Christianity, 'St. Ephrem's approach serves as a much needed antidote to that tradition of theologizing which seeks to provide theological definitions, Greek *horoi*, or boundaries. To Ephrem, theological definitions are not only potentially dangerous, but they can also be blasphemous.'[21] Likewise in ancient Egypt no particular interest is shown in defining terms, so famously there is no definition for *god*,[22] and most of the onomastic tradition has no attempt to define words until the Roman period, and even that is scanty.[23] There is no attempt to systematically set forth beliefs, and so no systematic theology. There is no catechetical literature; instructional literature assumes a common ground. An understanding of basic beliefs must be inferred from the texts. Assmann refers to this as 'implicit theology,'[24] but an implicit theology is one made explicit by outside observers and is not native to the religion.

(3) Since we are interested in ancient Egyptian interpretations of their own religion, passages where ancient Egyptians explain their religion are very important. A number of documents provide interpretations of ancient Egyptian religious documents by ancient Egyptians connected with the priestly hierarchies. These documents are insider interpretations and thus important and helpful in understanding what the Egyptians understood by certain expressions.

(4) Given a civilization comprising between two and five million people at any given time and that extended for at least three and a half millennia, it is probably possible to find just about any point of view. Absolutist statements practically beg for a counter-instance and it is often possible to find one. It is clear that different intellectual currents occurred in Ancient Egypt. In such circumstances, what we want are the common opinions. We should beware the isolated, unique documents at the expense of the ubiquitous documents or ideas. Book of the Dead 17 which occurs in more than 300 copies[25] is more important than Book of the Dead 175 which occurs in only eight.[26]

---

[19] Assmann, J., *The Search for God in Ancient Egypt*, trans. David Lorton, Ithaca, New York 2001, p. 9.
[20] Assmann, *The Search for God in Ancient Egypt*, p. 164.
[21] Brock, S., *The Luminous Eye: The Spiritual World Vision of Saint Ephrem the Syrian*, Kalamazoo, Michigan 1985, p. 23.
[22] Hornung, E., *Conception of God in Ancient Egypt: The One and the Many*, trans. John Baines, Ithaca, New York 1982, pp. 33-60.
[23] Osing, J., *Hieratische Papyri aus Tebtunis I* (= *CNI Publications* 17), Copenhagen 1998, pp. 40-42, 44.
[24] Assmann, *The Search for God in Ancient Egypt*, p. 8.
[25] See Quirke, S.G.J., *Owners of Funerary Papyri in the British Museum*, London 1993, p. 86 for a list of 51 copies.
[26] For this information I am grateful to the Totenbuch Projekt of Rheinische Friedrich-Wilhelms-Univerität Bonn.

(5) The final methodological point is that it is possible to have multiple interpretations for the same set of facts. As one philosopher put it: 'Historians often do not see any other interpretation which fits the facts as well as their own does; but if we consider that even in the field of physics, with its larger and more reliable stock of facts, new crucial experiments are needed again and again because the old ones are all in keeping with both of two competing and incompatible theories . . . then we shall give up the naïve belief that any definite set of historical records can ever be interpreted in one way only.'[27] When that happens, there may not be any particular way of deciding between competing interpretations. In theory one would prefer the theory that accounts for the most evidence, but in practice there might not be one. What I offer here is an alternative view to the standard one. While I think that the theory accounts for the evidence better than the alternatives, my colleagues will have the deciding say. I put it forward in the hope that it might prove a useful or insightful alternative.

Translations

It is often argued that the various parts of the human being have no translation into modern languages. This is ironic since most of them have translations into Egyptian or Greek made by ancient Egyptians who knew the languages and were adherents to the religion, and those terms do have standard translations into English. These translations, as we have noted, are important for comprehending the ancient Egyptian understanding of concepts and terms. It is also worth noting that the translations of various terms are not the only translations possible for the terms, nor do they cover all usages of the terms. After looking at how the terms have been translated, I will examine the way that the terms are used in Egyptian texts and how the translations work in those texts.

k3

One concept that is provided a translation by later Egyptians is the *k3*, which is 'uncommon in Demotic' and has all but disappeared.[28] The last use of the term is the second century A.D. Myth of the Sun's Eye.[29] Because the distinction between *q*, *k*, and *g* disappeared by at least the Twenty-Second Dynasty,[30] the noun *k3*, as a part of the human being,[31] became indistinguishable in pronunciation from *qi* 'image,'[32] *ky* 'other,'[33] and *k3* 'bull,'[34] with which it is regularly replaced

[27] Popper, K.R., *The Open Society and its Enemies*, 5th ed., New York 1967, p. 2:266; cf. Brock, *The Luminous Eye*, pp. 48-49: 'The number of possible interpretations is not finite. . . . It is not a case of one interpretation being right and another wrong (as can often be the case with historical exegesis).'

[28] Jasnow, R. and Zauzich, K.-Th., *The Ancient Egyptian Book of Thoth*, Wiesbaden 2005, p. 1:243; cf. *CDD* K (29 June 2001) 01:1:4-5; Quaegebeur, *Le dieu égyptien Shaï*, p. 135; cf. Smith, M., *The Mortuary Texts of Papyrus BM 10507* (=*Catalogue of Demotic Papyri in the British Museum* 3), London 1987, p. 181.

[29] P. Mythus 19/34, in de Cenival, F., *Le mythe de l'oeil du soleil* (=*Demotische Studien* 9), Sommerhausen 1988, pp. 60-61 and plate 19: *p3 4 k3.w n ḥ3.ṯ=y nḏm* 'the four kas of my heart are sweet.'

[30] See Jansen-Winkeln, K., *Spätmittelägyptische Grammatik der Texte der 3. Zwischenzeit* (=*ÄAT* 34), Wiesbaden 1996, p. 37.

[31] The term shows up in cuneiform transcriptions of names as *ku-ú*, in Greek transcriptions of names as γαω, κω, χου, χυ, χω, κο, and in Coptic transcriptions as Sahidic **ⲕⲟⲓ**, **ⲕⲓ**, **ⲭⲟⲓ**, **ⲭⲓ**, and **ⲭⲁⲓ**, Akhmimic **ⲕⲁⲓ**, Fayyumic **ⲕⲓ** and **ⲭⲓ**, and Bohairic **ⲭⲟⲓ**; see *Wb.* V 86, 93; *Demotisches Namesbuch*, 9:619, 624, 8:590, 9:620; Crum, W.E. *A Coptic Dictionary*, Oxford 1939, p. 133; Osing, J., *Die Nominalbildung des Ägyptischen*, Mainz am Rhein 1976, pp. 2:379-80; *CAD* K 497; Z 9; EA 14 III 43, 54, in Knudtzon, J.A., *Die El-Amarna-Tafeln*, Leipzig 1915, p. 1:120.

[32] The term *qi* 'image,' has a variety of pronunciations in Coptic, including Sahidic **ϭⲓ**, and **ⲅⲓ**, Lycopolitan **ϭⲓ**, and **ϫⲓ**, Akhmimic **ϭⲓ**, **ϭⲉ**, and **ϫⲉ**, Fayyumic **ϭⲓ**, **ϫⲓ**, **ϫⲉ**, and **ϭⲏ**, Bohairic **ϫⲉ**, and Mesokemic **ϭⲏ**; see Crum,

in Demotic personal names.[35] As a result of the phonetic confusion, later Egyptians sometimes found it expedient to translate the term in Egyptian. The early Roman period bilingual Rhind papyri, written for the offspring of a prophet of Hermonthes,[36] translate the hieratic *k3* generally by *rn* 'name,'[37] but also once by *šy* 'fortune.'[38] The connection of *k3* with 'name' occurs at least as early as the Twenty-Second Dynasty and spellings with a cartouche determinative appear frequently in Ptolemaic texts.[39] In fact, 'unless the sense is clear or determinative added it can be difficult to decide if ka or name is meant and the ambiguity is no doubt deliberate suggesting the ka and name were one entity.'[40] It is not certain that efforts to distinguish between *k3* and *rn* in the late period are necessarily meaningful; although the phonetic confusion with *qi* 'image' might be related to the supposed association of *k3* with an image.[41] The term *k3* is commonly replaced by *šy* 'fate' in the Ptolemaic and Roman periods,[42] and perhaps as early as the Eighteenth Dynasty.[43] In the Ptolemaic period, *k3* is sometimes replaced by *ʿḥʿ* 'lifetime,' *ʿḥʿ-nfr* 'good life,' *wḏḏ* 'what is decreed,' and *rnn.t* 'good fortune.'[44] Several of these terms are found in Amenemhet's list of extrinsic characteristics of the human being.

Also, in considering the term *k3*, we must be careful to distinguish the use of this term from the compound preposition *n-k3-(n)* which translates into Greek as εἰς, because 'this formula is often equivalent to the simple *n=s*,'[45] or a 'pleonastic expression for the simple *n*,' a fact that has been recognized independently and repeatedly.[46] The phrase had become lexicalized already in the Old Kingdom. The expression *n-k3-(n)* need not be anything more than a compound preposition meaning something like 'for the sake of, in behalf of, in memory of, to the name of.' Its usage, on numerous grave stelae, need not indicate anything about an individual any more than the compound preposition *m-b3ḥ* 'in the presence of' but literally 'in the foreskin of'[47] before a woman need indicate anything about her anatomy.[48] Indeed, one is hard pressed outside the phrase to find indication that an individual possesses a *k3*, particularly after the Old Kingdom.

The term *k3* can be plausibly linked to the verb *k3i* 'to think,' which applies to the past in the sense of 'to remember,' and to the future in the sense 'to plot, plan'[49] The passive participle of

---

Coptic Dictionary, Oxford 1939, 252; Schenke, H.-M., *Matthäus-Evangelium im Mitteläg ypotischen Dialekt des Koptischen (Codex Scheide)*, Berlin 1981, p. 165.

[33] The term *ky* 'other' has several pronunciations in Coptic, including Old Coptic ⲔⲈ, Sahidic ⲔⲈ, ϬⲈ, and ⲔⲞⲨ, Lycopolitan ⲔⲈ and ⲔⲀⲒ, Akhmimic ⲔⲈ, Mesokemic ⲔⲈ, ⲔⲎ and ⲔⲀⲒ, Fayyumic ⲔⲈ, ⲔⲎ, and ϬⲎ, and Bohairic ⲔⲈ; Crum, *Coptic Dictionary*, pp. 90-92; Schenke, *Matthäus-Evangelium im Mitteläg yptischen Dialekt*, p. 156.

[34] The term *k3* 'bull' appears in Old Coptic as ⲔⲞ; Crum, *Coptic Dictionary*, p. 92.

[35] *Demotisches Namensbuch* 8:590, 9:619-20, 624.

[36] Möller, G., *Die beiden Totenpapyrus Rhind des Museums zu Edinburg*, Leipzig 1913, pp. 7-8

[37] Möller, *Beiden Totenpapyrus Rhind*, p. 36*.

[38] Möller, *Beiden Totenpapyrus Rhind*, p. 54*; Quaegebeur, *Le dieu Shaï*, pp. 119, 134.

[39] *Wb.* V 92 ; Wilson, P., *A Ptolemaic Lexikon. A Lexicographical Study of the Ptolemaic Texts in the Temple of Edfu* (=*OLA* 78), Leuven 1997, p. 1079.

[40] Wilson, *Ptolemaic Lexikon*, p. 1079.

[41] Kurth, D. 'Zur Bedeutung des Ka-Names,' in: Kurth, D. (ed.), *Edfou VII*, Wiesbaden 2004, p. 671.

[42] Quaegebeur, *Le dieu égyptien Shaï*, p. 134.

[43] Quaegebeur, *Le dieu égyptien Shaï*, pp. 135-36, citing Sandman, M., *Texts from the Time of Akhenaten* (=*BAe* 8), Bruxelles 1938, p. 25; for a translation, see Murnane, W.J., *Texts from the Amarna Period in Egypt*, Atlanta 1995, p. 172.

[44] Quaegebeur, *Le dieu égyptien Shaï*, p. 136.

[45] Daumas, F., *Les moyens d'expression du grec et de l'égyptien*, Caire 1952, p. 14.

[46] Schweitzer, U., *Das Wesen des Ka in Diesseits und Jenseits der Alter Ägypter* (=*ÄF* 19), Glückstadt 1956, p. 82; Quaegebeur, *Le dieu égyptien Shaï*, p. 134.

[47] *Wb.* I 419-21.

[48] E.g. *m-b3ḥ=s* in P. Wien inv. Nr. 3862, in Satzinger, H., *Das Kunsthistorisches Museum im Wien: Die Ägyptisch-Orientalishe Sammlung*, Mainz 1994, p. 34.

[49] For a clear use of *k3i* in this sense, see Sethe, K., *Die Ächtung feindlicher Fürsten, Völker und Dinge auf altägyptischen Tongefässscherben des Mittleren Reiches*, Berlin 1926, p. 72, Tafel 29; Koenig, Y., 'Les textes d'envoûtement de Mirgissa,' *RdE* 41 (1990), pp. 119 (line 20), 125 (line 7); the Book of the Cow, in Hornung, E.,

this can have the appropriate vocalization[50] to account for the vocalizations of *kꜣ* attested,[51] and thus would mean 'what was remembered or thought' about someone in the past, or 'what is planned' for someone in the future. This on the one hand is the remembrance of an individual after death, thus 'may his *ka* [i.e. memory] dwell in the presence of the king'[52] which applies by extension to the memorial offerings (*kꜣ*) for a person, and, in abstract fashion to the nourishment they supply (*kꜣ.w*), and is most succinctly summed up in the name (*kꜣ*) of the individual. On the other hand, the *kꜣ* is what is decreed (*wḏd*) for the individual into the future and thus the individual's lifetime (*ꜥḥꜥw*), fate (*šꜣy*), and good fortune (*rnn.t*). Thus interpreting the noun *kꜣ* as the passive participle of the verb *kꜣi* can account for both the vocalization and the interpretations of the term. But such an interpretation means that the *kꜣ* is the memory or fate of a persona and not a division of the human being.

bꜣ

Like the term *kꜣ*, *bꜣ* also has its origins in a verbal root, one meaning 'to be manifest.'[53] This sense is preserved in the plural *bꜣ.w* (Coptic **ⲃⲉⲓ**)[54] 'manifestation,' specifically a manifestation of 'divine intervention in the everyday affairs of humans.'[55] The *bꜣ* is translated in bilingual mummy labels both as ονομα 'name,'[56] αυτην 'self,'[57] and ειδωλον 'ghost, image,'[58] with the plural given as μετα δοξης 'with glory.'[59] Egyptian rituals written in Greek tend to use the term παρεδρος 'assistant, attendant' to translate *bꜣ*.[60] The formula from Egyptian grave stele *ꜥnḫ pꜣy=f by m-bꜣḥ wsir nṯr ꜥꜣ nb ꜣbḏw* 'may his *bꜣ* live in the presence of Osiris, the great god, lord of Abydos'[61] is replaced in Greek by εὐψυχεῖ or ἀναπαύσον τὴν ψυχὴν αὐτοῦ εἰς κόλποις Ἀβρααμ

Der ägyptische Mythos von der Himmelskuh: Eine Ätiologie des Unvollkommenen, Freiburg, Schweiz and Göttingen 1982, p. 1.

[50] Osing, *Nominalbildung des Ägyptischen*, p. 1:238.

[51] Osing, *Nominalbildung des Ägyptischen*, p. 2:380.

[52] Tomb of Herymeru architrave, line 3, in Hassan, S., *Mastabas of Princess Hemet-Rꜥ and Others*, Cairo 1975, pp. 76-77, plate LVI; Strudwick, N., *Texts from the Pyramid Age*, Atlanta 2005, p. 219.

[53] Ward, *Four Egyptian Homographic Roots B-ꜣ*, pp. 72-73; Sauneron, S., 'Remarques de philologie et d'étymologie (§§ 19-25),' *RdE* 15 (1963), pp. 49-51.

[54] Osing, J., *Der spätägyptische Papyrus BM 10808* (=ÄA 33), Wiesbaden 1976, pp. 106-8, 232 n. 854, 249, citing Osing, *Nominalbildungen des Ägyptischen*, pp. 1:78-96.

[55] Borghouts, J.F., 'Divine Intervention in Ancient Egypt and its Manifestation (*bꜣw*),' in: Demarée, R.J., and Janssen J.J. (eds.), *Gleanings from Deir el-Medîna* (=*Egyptologische Uitgaven* 1), Leiden 1982, pp. 31-35.

[56] London, University College SB 3 7108, cited in Quaegebeur, J., 'Mummy Labels: An Orientation,' in: Boswinkel E., and Pestman, P.W., *Textes grecs, démotiques et bilingues (P. L. Bat. 19)*, Leiden 1978, p. 252.

[57] Louvre E 9595 = CEML no. 67, cited in Quaegebeur, 'Mummy Labels,' in: Boswinkel and Pestman, *Textes grecs, démotiques et bilingues*, p. 253.

[58] Louvre 611 = CEML no. 245, cited in Quaegebeur, 'Mummy Labels,' in: Boswinkel and Pestman, *Textes grecs, démotiques et bilingues*, p. 253; *LSJ* 483.

[59] Louvre 148 = CEML no. 356, cited in Quaegebeur, 'Mummy Labels,' in: Boswinkel and Pestman, *Textes grecs, démotiques et bilingues*, pp. 253-54.

[60] Gee, J., '*Bꜣ* Sending and Its Implications,' in: Hawass, Z. (ed.), *Egyptology at the Dawn of the Twenty-first Century*, Cairo 2003, pp. 2:230-37.

[61] For discussions, see Gee, J., "A New Look at the *ꜥnḫ pꜣ by* Formula," Spiegelberg, W., *Aegyptische und griechische Eigennamen aus Mumienetiketten der römischen Kaiserzeit*, Leipzig 1901, pp. 3-14; Möller, G., *Mumienschilder*, Leipzig 1913, pp. 4-5; Quaegebeur, 'Mummy Labels,' in: Boswinkel and Pestman, *Textes grecs, démotiques et bilingues*, pp. 232-59; Quaegebeur, J., 'P. Brux. Dem. E. 8258. Une letter de recommendations pour l'au-delà,' in: Groll, S.I. (ed.), *Studies in Egyptology Presented to Miriam Lichtheim*, Jerusalem 1990, pp. 2:776-95; Brunsch, B.W., 'Zwei funeräre demotische Texte in München (Staatliche Sammlung Ägyptischer Kunst Inv. Nr. 834 a/834 b),' in *Studien zu Sprache und Religion Ägyptens. Zu Ehren von Wolfhart Westendorf überreicht von seinen Freunden and Schülern*, Göttingen 1984, pp. 1:455-63; Thissen, H.J. *Die demotischen Graffiti von Medinet Habu: Zeugnisse zu Tempel und Kult im ptolemäischen Ägypten* (=*Demotische Studien* 10), Somerhausen 1989, pp. 196-97; Abdalla, A., *Graeco-Roman Funerary Stelae from Upper Egypt*, Liverpool 1992, pp. 121-23; Porten B., and Gee, J., 'Aramaic Funerary Practices in Egypt,' in: ed. Daviau, P.M.M. Weavers, J.W.

κ(αὶ) Ἰσαακ κ(αὶ) Ἰακωβ ‘rest his soul in the bosom of Abraham and Isaac and Jacob.’[62] So there is a clear use of ψυχή for *bꜣ*, it was not simply something out of Horapollo.[63] Žabkar notes this switch but concludes that ‘the Egyptians found the word *bꜣ* inadequate to express the Christian idea of soul.’[64] but given the Christian demonizing of many Egyptian concepts,[65] it might be more of a repudiation of the Egyptian religion rather than inadequacy of language.

ꜣḫ

The term *ꜣḫ*, like *kꜣ* and *bꜣ*, derives from a verb, in this case *ꜣḫ* ‘to be effective.’[66] Osing notes that the vocalization pattern is typically used for living things, meaning something like ‘an effective being.’[67] For the *ꜣḫ*, we know from Chalcidius’s commentary on Plato’s *Timaeus* that in the classical world it was thought that the Egyptians called the stars ‘Ach.’[68] But Chalcidius was a fourth century Christian commentator living in Italy,[69] and his knowledge cannot have been firsthand. This report does have its basis in the ancient Egyptian pun between *ꜣḫ*, which comes from the root meaning ‘to be effective,’ and *i͗ꜣḫ* ‘to be luminous,’ as texts pun between the entity *ꜣḫ* and *i͗ꜣḫ* referring to a star or planet.[70] There is evidence for a translation of this term into Greek by native Egyptian priests, but this will require a look at the function of an *ꜣḫ* first.

The Akh

More common than Amenemhet’s unique list of the supposed parts of the human being and therefore more pertinent to understanding ancient Egyptian religion are lists of types of beings. The same lists appear again and again from the Middle Kingdom through the Roman period. The terms *nṯr* and *ꜣḫ* are sometimes paired in the Pyramid Texts.[71] The list of *nṯr*, *ꜣḫ*, and *mwt* occurs no less than 17 times in the Coffin Texts,[72] seven times with *rmṯ* ‘man’ included at the

---

and Weigl, M. (eds.), *The World of the Arameans II: Studies in History and Archaeology in Honour of Paul-Eugène Dion*, Sheffield, England 2001, pp. 270-307; Stadler, M.A., ‘Fünf neue funeräre Kurztexte (Papyri Britisches Museum EA 10121, 10198, 10415, 10421a, b, 10426a) und eine Zwischenbilanz zu dieser Textgruppe,’ in: Hoffmann, F. and Thissen, H.-J. (eds.), *Res Severa Verum Gaudium. Festschrift für Karl-Theodor Zauzich zum 65. Geburtstag am 8. Juni 2004*, Leuven 2004, pp. 551-71.

[62] BM 1360, in Hall, H.R., *Coptic and Greek Texts of the Christian Period from Ostaka, Stelae, etc. in the British Museum*, London 1905, p. 12, and pl. 11. Compare BM 408, 602, 939, in Hall, *Coptic and Greek Texts of the Christian Period*, p. 10, 3.

[63] As maintained by Quaegebeur, ‘Mummy Labels,’ in: Boswinkel and Pestman, *Textes grecs, démotiques et bilingues*, pp. 252-54. Horopollo, *Hieroglyphica* I.7 does equate ψυχή with βαι: ἐστι γὰρ μὲν τὸ βαι ψυχή.

[64] Žabkar, *A Study of the Ba Concept in Ancient Egyptian Texts*, p. 162.

[65] For example the shift from *ꜣḫ* “angel” to ⲓϩ “demon,” *i͗mnt.t* “dwelling place of the angels” to ⲁⲙⲉⲛⲧⲉ “hell, dwelling place of the damned.” While the Christians might keep some general concepts, like *nṯr* > ⲛⲟⲩⲧⲉ “God” as a rival religion competing for the salvation of the human soul, concepts for individual salvation needed different branding.

[66] Friedman, F., ‘The Root Meaning of *ꜣḫ*: Effectiveness or Luminosity,’ *Serapis* 8 (1985), pp. 39-46; K. Jansen-Winkeln, ‘“Horizont” und “Verklärtheit”. Zur Bedeutung der Wurzel *ꜣḫ*’, *SAK* 23 (1996), pp. 201-215.

[67] Osing, *Nominalbildung des Ägyptischen*, pp. 1:193, cf. 2:569 n. 446, 2:721 n. 845.

[68] Chalcidius, *Comm. ad Platon. Tim.* 126, in Hopfner, T., *Fontes historiae religionis aegyptiacae*, Bonn 1922-1924, pp. 512-13.

[69] Chadwick, H., “C(h)alcidius,” in: Hammond, N.G.L. and Scollard, H.H. (eds.), *The Oxford Classical Dictionary*, 2nd ed., Oxford 1970, 226.

[70] Thus *ntf pw i͗my.w-ꜣḫ i͗my.w-i͗ꜣḫ* “he is among the *ꜣḫ*s and among the stars” BD 78, in Lepsius, R. *Das Totenbuch der Ägypter nach dem hieroglyphischen Papyrus in Turin*, Leipzig 1842, Tafel XXVIII.

[71] PT 217 § 153; 222 §§ 204, 206; 422 § 763; 478 § 980.

[72] CT 47 I 207, 131 II 152, 165 III 8, 282 IV 32, 455 V 327, 472 VI 1, 477 VI 35 (twice), 477 VI 36, 507 VI 93 (twice), 585 VI 203 (twice), 585 VI 204, 647 VI 269, 672 VI 300, 772 VI 406.

beginning of the list.[73] In the Book of the Dead, the *nṯr.w* and the *3ḫ.w* are paired eight times,[74] and the list of *nṯr*, *3ḫ*, and *mwt* also occurs twelve times in the Book of the Dead,[75] seven times with *rmṯ* 'man' included at the beginning of the list.[76] The list of four occurs four times in the solar hymns,[77] where there are also three additional pairings of *3ḫ* and *nṯr*,[78] and one each of *rmṯ* and *nṯr*,[79] *rmṯ* and *3ḫ*,[80] and *3ḫ* and *mwt*.[81] The triple list also occurs elsewhere.[82] The sequence *rmṯ* 'humans,' *nṯr.w* 'gods,' *3ḫ.w* and *mwt.w* 'the damned,' seems to be a list of the types of beings for the ancient Egyptians.[83] I have argued elsewhere that the term *b3* subsumes the categories of *nṯr.w* 'gods,' *3ḫ.w* and *mwt.w* 'the damned,'[84] and that a *nṯr* can be said to be a *b3*,[85] (it is also said to be an *3ḫ*),[86] an *3ḫ* can be said to be a *b3*,[87] and a *mwt* can be said to be a *b3*,[88] but this can be confirmed with a papyrus that explicitly lists *n3 by n nṯr n3 by n rmṯ.t n3 by n t3 dw3.t n3 by n t3 iḫy.t n3 iyḫ.w n3 in-mwt* 'the *b3*s of the gods, the *b3*s of men, the *b3*s of the netherworld, the *b3*s of the horizon, the *3ḫ*s and the damned.'[89] In this way the *b3* is the larger category of being while men, the gods, the akhs and the damned are the subcategories.

In Old Kingdom inscriptions, officials want to become an *3ḫ* and not a *b3*.[90] The term is parallel to the lector priest,[91] and both were noted for their knowledge of secrets (*sšt3*), powers (*ḥk3*) and texts (*r3*).[92] An *3ḫ* is a being for whom all the proper rituals have been performed.[93]

---

[73] CT 165 III 8, 455 V 327, 477 VI 35 (twice), 477 VI 36, 507 VI 93, 647 VI 269.

[74] BD 78, 82, 125 A 18-19, 126, 130, 136, 141, 149 (ninth mound), in Lepsius, *Das Totenbuch der Ägypter*, Tafel XXIX, XXXI, XLVI, LI, LIII, LVI, LVIII, LXXII; Maystre, C., *Les déclarations d'innocence (Livre des morts, chapitre 125)*, Caire 1937, pp. 39-40.

[75] BD 42, 130, 133, 148, 149 (sixth mound), 149 (ninth mound), 149 (eleventh mound), 152, in Lepsius, *Totenbuch der Ägypter*, Tafel XIX, LIV, LVI, LXIX, LXXI, LXXII, LXXIV; BD 134, 136A, 137, 175, BD 167 Pleyte.

[76] BD 42, 130, 148, 152, in Lepsius, *Totenbuch der Ägypter*, Tafel XIX, LIV, LXIX, LXXIV; BD 134, 175, BD 167 Pleyte.

[77] Sonnenhymnen 40.16-17, 87.10-11, 156.51-52, 213.16-17, in Assmann, J., *Sonnenhymnen in thebanischen Gräbern*, Mainz am Rhein 1983, pp. 54-55, 123, 204, 294.

[78] Sonnenhymnen 37.36-37, 121.4, 212a.5-6, in Assmann, *Sonnenhymnen in thebanischen Gräbern*, pp. 49, 166, 290.

[79] Sonnenhymn 37.34, in Assmann, *Sonnenhymnen in thebanischen Gräbern*, p. 49.

[80] Sonnenhymn 61.7-9, in Assmann, *Sonnenhymnen in thebanischen Gräbern*, p. 88.

[81] Sonnenhymn 156.2, in Assmann, *Sonnenhymnen in thebanischen Gräbern*, p. 203.

[82] P. Harkness 2/35-36, in Smith, M., *Papyrus Harkness (MMA 31.9.7)*, Oxford 2005, pp. 63-64.

[83] Gee, '*B3* Sending and Its Implications,' in: Hawass (ed.), *Egyptology at the Dawn of the Twenty-first Century*, pp. 2:230-37.

[84] Gee, '*B3* Sending and Its Implications,' in: Hawass (ed.), *Egyptology at the Dawn of the Twenty-first Century*, pp. 2:230-37.

[85] 26-31: PT 217 §§ 152-60, 306 §§ 478-79; 482 §§ 1004-5; 505 § 1089; 555 § 1373; 670 §§ 1973-74; CT 154 II 286-87, 155 II 306-9, 156 II 322-25, 157 II 348, 158 II 361-62, 159 II 371-72, 160 II 386-87; BD 109, 112-16; Žabkar, *Study of the Ba Concept in Ancient Egyptian Texts*, pp. 12-15, 28-30.

[86] BD 60, in Lepsius, *Totenbuch der Ägypter*, Tafel XXIII.

[87] CT 384 V 49, 51.

[88] CT 384 V 51 vs. BD 30B, 125.

[89] P. Mag. 9/21-22, repeated in 9/35-10/1 with the variation of *n3 mty* for *n3 in-mwt*, in Griffith, F.Ll. and Thompson, H., *The Demotic Magical Papyrus of London and Leiden*, London 1904-6, 2:pls. IX-X.

[90] *Urk.* I 79, 116, 122, 143, 202, 218, 219, 224, 263, 269; Cairo 20539; Louvre C 15; Edel, E., 'Untersuchungen zur Phraseologie der ägyptischen Inschriften des Alten Reiches,' *MDAIK* 13 (1944), pp. 19-21.

[91] *Urk.* I 89, 122, 197, 202, 256; Edel, *MDAIK* 13 (1944), pp. 19-21.

[92] *Urk.* I 116, 117, 142-43, 173, 186, 218, 256, 263; Cairo 20539; Louvre C 14; PT 77 § 52; Edel, *MDAIK* 13 (1944), pp. 22-26; Elmar Edel, 'Zum Verständnis der Inschrift des *Jzj* aus Saqqara,' *ZÄS* 106 (1979), pp. 105-16; Demarée, R.J., *The 3ḫ iḳr n Rʿ-Stelae: On Ancestor Worship in Ancient Egypt*, Leiden 1983, pp. 193-94, 200-1, 203-6, 208, 224-25, 239, 243-44, 277; Barta, W., *Die Bedeutung der Pyramidentexte für den verstorbene König*, München 1981, pp. 62-64, 104-5.

[93] *Urk.* I 173, 187, 263; CT 158 II 360, 760 VI 390, 116 VII 447, 1117 VI 448, 1131 VII 474; BD 17, 113, 148; Amduat, 2nd hour, 3rd hour, 11th hour; Tomb of *wsr-nṯr*, in Murray, M.A., *Saqqara Mastabas, Part I*, London 1905, pl. XXIII; Edel, *MDAIK* 13 (1944), pp. 26-30; Englund, G., *Akh – une notion religieuse dans l'Égypte pharaonique*, Uppsala 1978, pp. 108-9, 158, 192.

These rituals are contained in the *s3ḫw* texts,[94] explicitly identified in both the Coffin Texts[95] and the Book of the Dead.[96] (As a side note, there also appears to be an equivalent *sb3* literature which we tend to refer to as wisdom or instructional literature.)[97] In this way the *b3* is said to be an *3ḫ*: "Make way for my *b3* since my shade (*šw.t*) is in me and I am equipped. I am an equipped *3ḫ*."[98] The *3ḫ* is also said to have a *b3*: 'As for every *3ḫ* for whom this scroll is done, his *b3* will go forth by day among the living.'[99]

Coffin Texts discussing the sending of the *b3* have their parallel in Roman times with texts from a Theban temple archive discussing sending of messengers to appear in dreams, or sending assistants.[100] These assistants are described as θεοί, ἄγγελοι, or δαίμονες,[101] and the three categories correspond to the division of the categories of *b3* into the *nṯr*, the *3ḫ*, and the *mwt*, providing us with Greek translations for these categories and standard English equivalents of the categories: gods, angels, and demons. While the term *angel* carries significant baggage in the Western tradition, any term used in translation carries undesirable baggage. It is therefore worth comparing the use of the term ἄγγελος from this archive with the earlier Egyptian texts describing the capabilities of the *3ḫ*. The comparison is not exact, but quite close. One of the texts describes the capabilities of the ἄγγελος, or πνεῦμα ἀέριον:

> ὀνειροπομπεῖ, ἄγει γυναῖκας, ἄνδρας δία οὐσιας, ἀναιρεῖ, καταστ[ρ]έφει, ἀναρίπτει ἀνέμους ἐκ γῆς, βασταζει χρυσον ἄργυρον, χαλκόν, καὶ δίδωσι σοι, ὅταν χρεία γένηται, λύει δὲ ἐκ δεσμῶν [ἁ]λύσεσι φρουρούμενον, θύρας ἀνοίγει, ἀμαυροῖ ἵνα μηδεὶς [κ]αθόλου θεωρήσῃ, πυρφορεῖ, ὕδωρ φέρει, οἶνον, ἄρτον καὶ [ὃ] ἂν ἐθέλεις ἐκ τῶν ἐδεσμάτων, ἔλαιον, ὄξος, χωρὶς ἰχθύων μ[ό]νων, λαχάνων δὲ πλῆθος, ὃ θέλεις, ἄξει . . . κα[ὶ ὁπόταν αὐτὸν] κελεύσῃς διακο[ῦσαι], ποιήσει, καὶ ὄψῃ προ[τερή]σαντα ἄλλοις. ἵστησι πλοῖα καὶ πά[λιν] ἀπολύει, ἵστησι πονηρὰ δαιμόνια πλεῖστα, θῆρας δὲ παύει καὶ ὀδόντας ῥήξει ἑρπετ[ῶν ἀν]ημέρων συντόμως, κύνας δὲ κοιμίζει καὶ ἀφώνο[υς ἵσ]τησι, μεταμορφοῖ δὲ εἰς ἣν ἐὰν βούλῃ μορφὴν θη[ρίου], πετηνοῦ, ἐνύδρου, τετραπόδου, ἑρπετοῦ. βαστάξει σ[ε εἰς] ἀέρα καὶ παλιν ῥίψει σε εἰς κλύδωνα ποντίων ποταμῶν καὶ εἰς ῥύ<α>κας θαλσσίων, πήξει δὲ ποταμοὺς καὶ θάλασσα[ν συντ]όμως καὶ, ὅπως ἐνδιατρέχῃς σταδίως, ὡς βούλει. . . . λύχνους ἀνά[ψει κ]αὶ κατασβέσει πάλιν.

> 'he sends dreams, leads women and men without substances, kills, destroys, hurls winds up out of the earth, carries gold, silver and bronze, and gives them to you when the need arises, loosens the bonds of those fettered in prison, opens doors, makes invisible so that no one can see you at all, brings fire, water, wine, bread, whatever you wish in the way of food, olive oil, vinegar–just not fish–lots of vegetables, he will bring what you want, . . . and [whatever] you command [him to] do, he will do, and you will see him excelling in other ways; he stops ships and again releases them, he stops most evi[l demon]s, halts beasts and suddenly breaks fierce reptiles' teeth, puts dogs to sleep and silences them, changes into whatever form you want, b[east], bird, fish, four-footed beast, reptile. He will carry [you into] the air, and again, cast you into the waves of the sea or river, and into the

[94] Sonnenhymnen 52.64, 74.27, 123.18, in Assmann, *Sonnenhymnen in thebanischen Gräbern*, pp. 68, 70, 109, 168; Assmann, J., *Images et rites de la mort dans l'Égypte ancienne: L'apport des liturgies funéraires*, Paris 2000, pp. 81-92.
[95] CT 1 I 1.
[96] BD 1, 100, 130, 133-34, 136, 141-42, 190.
[97] Redford, D.B., *Pharaonic King-Lists, Annals and Day Books: A Contribution to the Study of the Egyptian Sense of History*, Mississauga 1986, p. 217 n. 54.
[98] BD 91, in Lepsius, *Totenbuch der Ägypter*, Tafel XXXIII.
[99] BD 148, in Lepsius, *Totenbuch der Ägypter*, Tafel LXIX.
[100] Ciraolo, L.J., 'Supernatural Assistants in the Greek Magical Papyri,' in: Meyer, M. and Mirecki, P. (eds.), *Ancient Magic and Ritual Power*, Leiden 1995, pp. 279-95.
[101] Ciraolo, 'Supernatural Assistants in the Greek Magical Papyri,' in: Meyer and Mirecki (eds.), *Ancient Magic and Ritual Power*, pp. 279-93.

waves of the sea, he will freeze rivers and the sea suddenly even, so that you can run across if you like, . . . he will light lamps and extinguish them.'[102]

These are all features of the *3ḫ*, who had power over the damned,[103] and the living,[104] could cause health,[105] sickness,[106] childbirth,[107] financial distress,[108] or general malady.[109] They could also send dreams,[110] lead men and women,[111] do work,[112] fight demons, light lamps,[113] kill,[114] move ships,[115] transform themselves into lotuses,[116] barley,[117] falcons,[118] phoenixes,[119] herons,[120] geese,[121] swallows,[122] ibises,[123] vultures,[124] other birds,[125] bulls,[126] crocodiles,[127] snakes,[128] spirits,[129] gods,[130] fire,[131] air,[132] whatever form desired,[133] and in that form they could appear in various places, to whomever they wished.[134] They open doors,[135] travel through fire,[136] loose bonds,[137] drive away

---

[102] *PGM* I 98-127.

[103] Hu Bowl 3-5, in Gardiner, A.H. and Sethe, K., *Egyptian Letters to the Dead Mainly from the Old and Middle Kingdoms*, London 1928, plates IV-IVA.

[104] Demarée, *The 3ḫ iḳr n Rᶜ-Stelae*, p. 277.

[105] OIM 13945 4, in Gardiner, A.H., 'A New Letter to the Dead,' *JEA* 16 (1930), pp. 19-20; *Urk.* I 202; Demarée, *The 3ḫ iḳr n Rᶜ-Stelae*, pp. 210-11.

[106] Cairo CG 25375 2-4, in Gardiner and Sethe, *Egyptian Letters to the Dead*, pp. 7-8, plates VI-VIA; Bentresh Stele (Louvre C 284) 9-12, in de Buck, A., *Egyptian Readingbook*, Leiden 1963, p. 107.

[107] OIM 13945 4, in Gardiner, 'New Letter to the Dead,' pp. 19-20; Demarée, *The 3ḫ iḳr n Rᶜ-Stelae*, p. 215.

[108] Cairo JE 25975 4-9, in Gardiner and Sethe, *Egyptian Letters to the Dead*, plates I-IA.

[109] Berlin bowl, in Gardiner and Sethe, *Egyptian Letters to the Dead*, plates V-VA; Demarée, *The 3ḫ iḳr n Rᶜ-Stelae*, pp. 194, 269-70.

[110] CT 89 II 55, 98-101 II 93-105, 103-104 II 110-12; Gee, J., 'Oracle by Image: Coffin Text 103 in Context,' in: Ciraolo, L., and Seidel, J. (eds.), *Magic and Divination in the Ancient World*, Leiden 2002, pp. 83-88; Gee, '*B3* Sending and Its Implications,' in: Hawass (ed.), *Egyptology at the Dawn of the Twenty-first Century*, pp. 230-37.

[111] P. Setna I 4/38-5/30.

[112] BD 5-6.

[113] BD 137, 137A, 137B.

[114] *Urk.* I 90, 142, 202; James, T.G.H., *The Mastaba of Khentika Called Ikhekhi*, London 1953, pp. 19-20, 37-38, plate V; Blumenthal, E., 'Die 'Reinheit' des Grabschänders,' in Verhoeven, U. and Graefe, E. (eds.), *Religion und Philosophie im alten Ägypten. Festgabe für Philippe Derchain zu seinem 65. Geburtstag am 24. Juli 1991* (= *OLA* 39), Leuven 1991, p. 47; Morschauser, S., *Threat-Formulae in Ancient Egypt*, Baltimore 1991, pp. 67-68, 79; Demarée, *The 3ḫ iḳr n Rᶜ-Stelae*, pp. 206-7.

[115] P. Setna I 3/27-30.

[116] BD 81A-B.

[117] CT 269 IV 6-7.

[118] CT 273-274 IV 11-15, 286 IV 36-38, 302 IV 53-55, 312-313 IV 68-93, 989 VII 197-99; BD 77-78.

[119] BD 83.

[120] CT 272 IV 10, 292 IV 43-44; BD 84.

[121] CT 278 IV 23-25, 287 IV 38-39.

[122] CT 283 IV 33, 293-294 IV 45-47, 678 VI 305; BD 86.

[123] CT 386 V 53.

[124] CT 955 VII 169-70.

[125] CT 271 IV 9, 703 VI 334-35.

[126] CT 208 III 161-62.

[127] PT 317 §§507-10; CT 268 IV 1-5, 285 IV 35-36, 991 VII 201-3; BD 88.

[128] CT 374 V 37; BD 87.

[129] BD 85.

[130] PT 317 §§ 507-10; CT 252 III 352, 256 III 365-66, 261 III 382-89, 268 IV 1-5, 270 IV 8, 276-277 IV 17-22, 280-282 IV 28-32, 285 IV 35-36, 290 IV 42, 301 IV 52-53, 316-317 IV 98-135, 322 IV 148-51, 325-326 IV 154-62, 330-331 IV 166-76, 464-467 V 336-78, 546-547 VI 142-43, 612 VI 225-26, 669 VI 297, 712 VI 343, 957 VII 172-76, 991 VII 201-3, 993 VII 205-7, 1016 VII 235; BD 79-80, 82, 88; Louvre E 3229 5/2-6, in Johnson, J.H., 'Louvre E 3229,' *Enchoria* 7 (1977), p. 63, Tafel 14; *PGM* I 73-95.

[131] CT 284 IV 34, 316 IV 98-109.

[132] CT 288 IV 40.

[133] CT 275 IV 16, 573 VI 177-83, 794 VII 4, 829 VII 30; BD 17, 64 variant, 76; P. Setna I 5/31-36, 6/9-17, in Spiegelberg, W., *Die demostischen Denkmäler. II. Die demotische Papyrus*, Strassburg 1906, 2:pls. XLVI-XLVII.

[134] CT 99 II 103-5; 101-4 II 110-12; P. Setna I 6/2-3, in Spiegelberg, *Die demotische Papyrus*, 2:pl. XLVII; Griffith, *Stories of the High Priests of Memphis*, pp. 136-37.

crocodiles,[138] snakes,[139] vultures,[140] pigs,[141] cockroaches,[142] and other undesirable creatures,[143] control water,[144] winds,[145] fire,[146] and enemies,[147] and bring bread,[148] water,[149] beer,[150] and other foods.[151] The results of this comparison may be summed up in the following chart:

Items in common		
	ꜣḫ	ἄγγελος
Sends dreams	X	X
Leads men and women	X	X
Kills	X	X
Causes sickness	X	X
Causes financial distress	X	X
Hurls winds	X	X
Opens doors	X	X
Brings fire	X	X
Brings water	X	X
Brings bread	X	X
Brings food	X	X
Does commands	X	X
Stops demons	X	X
Stops beasts	X	X
Transforms into birds	X	X
Transforms into beasts	X	X
Transforms into fish	X	X
Transforms into reptiles	X	X
Freezes rivers	X	X
Lights lamps	X	X

[135] CT 242-43 III 327-31, 264 III 393, 323-24 IV 152-53, 645-46 VI 265-66, 1007 VII 223; BD 67, 92.
[136] CT 246-48 III 337-42; BD 63.
[137] CT 343 IV 348-64, 473 VI 3-16, 475-81 VI 26-47; BD 91, 153, 153B.
[138] CT 342 IV 346-47, 424 V 265-68, 586 VI 205-8; BD 31-32.
[139] CT 369 V 31, 378-79 V 41-43, 381-82 V 44, 434-36 V 283-89, 586 VI 205-8, 885 VII 94-98; BD 7, 33-35, 37, 39, 41B.
[140] CT 425 V 269-70, 430 V 277.
[141] CT 440 V 293-96.
[142] BD 36.
[143] CT 439 V 292, 441-43 V 297-109, 450 V 319, 452-54 V 322-36, 579 VI 194, 698 VI 332, 750 VI 379-80, 891 VII 101-2; BD 40-42.
[144] CT 353 IV 392-400, 356 V 8, 359 V 12-14, 361-62 V 15-22, 431 V 278-79, 451 V 320, 467 V 363-78, 820 VII 20-21, 994 VII 208-9, 1015 VII 233-34.
[145] CT 355 V 1-7, 676 VI 304.
[146] CT 799 VII 7, 1009 VII 224; BD 137, 137A, 137B, Pleyte 171.
[147] CT 569 VI 168-69, 799 VII 7; BD 10-11, 65, 134.
[148] CT 371 V 33-34, 421-22 V 258-60, 604 VI 218, 661 VI 287, 797 VII 5; BD 82.
[149] CT 353 IV 392-400, 356 V 8, 359 V 12-14, 361-362 V 15-22, 431 V 278-79, 451 V 320, 467 V 363-78, 1015 VII 233-34; BD 57-59, 62-63, 136.
[150] CT 604 VI 218; BD 82.
[151] CT 591 VI 211, 599 VI 215, 739 VI 367; BD 106, 136.

Elements unique to the *ꜣḫ*		
	ꜣḫ	*ἄγγελος*
Transforms into plants	X	
Transforms into gods	X	
Transforms into fire	X	
Heals	X	
Elements unique to the ἄγγελος		
Carries metal		X
Loosens bands		X
Makes invisible		X
Brings wine		X
Stops ships		X
Carries in air		X
Casts into water		X

The two categories have twenty elements in common and four or seven elements unique to them, but they also come from texts that are separated by as much as two millennia.

In English, the term *angel* is used to mean 'a ministering spirit or divine messenger; one of an order of spiritual beings superior to man in power and intelligence.'[152] Since in all cases under consideration, the messengers in the Egyptian texts represent 'spiritual beings superior to man in power and intelligence,' the use of the English term *angel* represents a suitable translation for the Egyptian term *ꜣḫ*.

The Ba

Žabkar opposes 'the dualistic opposition between the "body" and the "soul."'[153] Unfortunately for his thesis, there are numerous passages where the ba and the body are opposed, enough to discern a distinct pattern.[154] In the Pyramid Texts *bꜣ* "soul" and *ẖ.t* 'body' are opposed once,[155] and *bꜣ* 'soul' and *ḏ.t* 'body' are opposed twice,[156] while *bꜣ* 'soul' and *ỉwf* 'flesh' seem to be opposed twice.[157] In the Coffin Texts the opposition *bꜣ* 'soul' and *ẖꜣ.t* 'body' occurs five times,[158] and the opposition *bꜣ* 'soul' and *ḏ.t* 'body' occurs fourteen times.[159] In the Book of the Dead *bꜣ* 'soul' and *ḏ.t* 'body' are opposed twice.[160] In the Amduat *bꜣ* and *ẖꜣ.t* are opposed at least twice.[161] In the solar hymns, *bꜣ* and *ẖꜣ.t* are opposed four times,[162] *bꜣ* and *ḏ.t* twice,[163] and *bꜣ* and *ỉwf*

[152] *Oxford English Dictionary*, s.v. "angel."
[153] Žabkar, *A Study of the Ba Concept in Ancient Egyptian Texts*, p. 1.
[154] See also Sauneron, "Remarques de philologie et d'étymologie (§§ 19-25)," p. 49.
[155] PT 274 § 413.
[156] PT 506 § 1098; 690 § 2096.
[157] PT 555 § 1378; 676 § 2010; 690 § 2098.
[158] CT 20 I 56; 94 II 67; 229 III 296; 333 IV 178; 493 VI 73.
[159] CT 307 IV 63; 314 IV 96; 409 V 227-31; 413 V 243; 493 VI 74-75; 495 VI 77.
[160] BD 85, 89.
[161] Amduat I 57, 195/96.
[162] Sonnenhymnen 17.37-38, 40.8-9, 186.37-38, 217.5, in Assmann, *Sonnenhymnen in thebanischen Gräbern*, pp. 19, 55, 259, 300.
[163] Sonnenhymnen 38.32-33, 256.3-4, in Assmann, *Sonnenhymnen in thebanischen Gräbern*, pp. 51, 365.

'flesh' once.[164] This opposition between body and soul lasts through the Ptolemaic period.[165] It is not imposed upon the material by later Egyptologists; it comes from the ancient Egyptian texts themselves.

According to a recent exposition, 'at death, the ka separated from the body. In order for an individual to survive as a spirit in the afterlife, the ba had to be reunited with its ka, its life force: in the Pyramid Texts and elsewhere, the deceased are called "those who have gone to their kas." The resultant spiritual entity was known as an akh: literally, an "effective" being.'[166] Unfortunately, in no place in the Pyramid Texts, the Coffin Texts, or the Book of the Dead is it said that the *b3* unites with the *k3* under any circumstances.[167] Only in one passage is the *k3* said to be with the *b3*,[168] but the text is garbled even in the early versions and it is not clear what sort of weight one should place on a garbled text, which in any case discusses 'my ba' and 'your ka.'[169] Žabkar admits that 'the text is very awkwardly construed, the variants are of little help, and

[164] Sonnenhymn 196.10-11, in Assmann, *Sonnenhymnen in thebanischen Gräbern*, p. 275.

[165] *mkt tw=k ḫ3p-n-nb=s ḥnʿ nṯr ʿ3 ḥ3y=k ʿnḫ m ḏdw ṯ3-wr b3=k ʿnḫ m p.t* Document of Breathings Made by Isis §8 from P. Louvre N 3284 3/7-8, in Rhodes, M.D., *The Hor Book of Breathings: A Translation and Commentary*, Provo, Utah 2002, p. 56

[166] Allen, *Ancient Egyptian Pyramid Texts*, p. 7.

[167] The terms *b3* and *k3* occur together only four times in the Pyramid Texts: In PT 218 §162 individuals and their *k3*s are said not to be denied bread and this is done by someone who is *b3* (*b3.tj*); for the interpretation, see Allen, J.P., *The Ancient Egyptian Pyramid Texts*, Atlanta, 2005, p. 34. In the Cannibal Hymn, the king's *k3.w* are said to be around him (*ḥ3=f*) when he sees the *b3*; PT 273 §396. In PT 436 §789, glorification (*s3ḫ*) is said to occur for the sake of its *b3* (*n b3=f*), but then the narrative changes and discusses the deceased sitting down to a meal with his *k3* (*k3=k*) using a different personal pronoun. Finally, in the purification ritual in PT 451 §837, the individual, his *k3* and *b3* are said to be washed. The words *b3* and *k3* only occur together five times in the Coffin Texts, three of these instances in only a single coffin (CT 192 III 109, 840 VII 45, 841 VII 46.). In CT 45 I 193 we are told of an action done "on the day in which your *k3* and *b3* rest." In CT 192 III 109, *b3* is used as a textual variant in one coffin instead of *k3*. In CT 647 VI 268 we learn that Nehebkaw is the one "who gives *b3.w* (souls), *ḫʿ.w* (appearances), *k3.w* (memories), and *š3ʿ.w* (beginnings)." In CT 840 VII 45, the deceased is told "your *k3* is your protection; your *b3* is within you." In a broken text, CT 841 VII 46, it says "your *k3* and your *b3* are in [. . .]." The situation is not improved much by the Book of the Dead where the two are conjoined only two times: "I do what my *k3* wants; my *b3* will not be kept back from my body." (BD 26, in Lepsius, *Totenbuch der Ägypter*, Tafel XV.) BD 92 is discussed below.

[168] BD 92.

[169] A sample of manuscripts gives the following variants:

isy w3.t n=i k3=k ḥnʿ=k b3=i [. . .] "Go far away for me, your ka with you, my ba [. . .]." pNu (early Dynasty 18), in Lapp, G., *The Papyrus of Nu*, London 1997, pl. 19.

sby w3.t n=i n k3=k ḥnʿ=k b3=i 3ḫ=i ʿpr "Go far away for me and for your ka with you; my ba, my akh are equipped" *pJmn-ḥtp* Cc (Amenhotep II), in Munro, I., *Die Totenbuch-Handschriften der 18. Dynastie im Ägyptischen Museum Cairo* (=ÄA 54), Wiesbaden 1994, 2:Taf. 74.

isy w3.t [. . .] "Go far away [. . .]" *pJmn-ḥtp* Cd (Amenhotep II), in Munro, *Die Totenbuch-Handschriften der 18. Dynastie im Ägyptischen Museum Cairo*, 2 Taf. 103.

issy w3.t n=i n k3=k ḥnʿ=k m b3 "Go far away for me and for your ka with you as a ba" *pM3j-ḥr-prj* (Amenhotep II), in Munro, *Die Totenbuch-Handschriften der 18. Dynastie im Ägyptischen Museum Cairo*, 2:Taf. 122.

isy w3.t n k3=k ḥnʿ=k m b3 in iry.w ʿ.wt wsir "Go far away for your ka with you as a ba, said the keepers of the limbs of Osiris." pNb-snj (Tuthmosis IV), in Naville, E., *Das aegyptische Todtenbuch der XVIII. bis XX. Dynastie*, Berlin 1886, 1:Taf. CIV.

isy w3.t n=i n ib=k ḥnʿ=k b3=i 3ḫ ʿpr "Go far away for me and for your heart with you, my ba is an equipped akh" *p3ny* (Dynasty 19), in von Dassow, E., *The Egyptian Book of the Dead: The Book of Going Forth by Day*, San Francisco 1994, plate 17.

isb w3w=f n k3=k ḥnʿ=k b3=i 3ḫw=i ʿpr n sšm=sn tw "Go so that he may be far away for your ka and you; my ba, my akh is equipped for their guiding you" *pNs-p3-sfy*, in Verhoeven, U., *Das Totenbuch des Monthpriesters Nespasefy aus der Zeit Psammetichs I.* (=*Handschriften des Altägyptischen Totenbuches* 5), Wiesbaden 1999, Taf. 37.

iw sw3=i w3.t n=f n k3=k ḥnʿ=k b3 3ḫ.t ʿpr n sšm=sn "I pass by the road for him for his ka and you; the ba is an akh equipped for leading them." pCologny, in Munro, I., *Der Totenbuch-Papyrus des Hor aus der frühen Ptolemäerzeit (pCologny Bodmer-Stiftung CV + pCincinnati Art Museum 1947.369 + pDenver Art Museum 1954.61)* (=*Handschriften des Altägyptischen Totenbuches* 9), Wiesbaden 2006, Tafel 9.

the personal pronouns are confused,'[170] and yet he still constructs much of his understanding of the ba in the Book of the Dead on this passage. That is simply a modern myth retroactively applied to the ancient Egyptians and not something, so far as I have been able to tell, that they ever believed. In fact, Egyptian texts say the opposite. An inscription from the tomb of the Sixth Dynasty official Herymeru requests: 'may his *ka* dwell in the presence of the king, may his *ba* endure in the presence of the god'[171] So, at least in this case, the *k3* stays around with the mortal king while the *b3* goes off with the immortal gods. The *k3* is, for the most part, not associated with the other parts of the human being or categories of beings.

So if there are no ancient Egyptian texts that discuss the *b3* and the *k3* getting together to form an *3ḫ*, where does the idea come from? The earliest advancement of the theory of which I am aware is in Žabkar's book on the Ba-Concept, where he states 'when the king "dies" he goes to his Ka, as the gods did, to or with his Ba, and he becomes an Akh.'[172] Žabkar simply asserts this proposition without supporting it with references or argumentation. The assertion is problematic for a number of reasons: One is that gods[173] and akhs are said to go to their *k3*s,[174] so this can hardly be a condition for becoming an *3ḫ*. Another is that the phrase *sbi n k3* 'to go to one's fate' is simply used as a euphemism for dying.[175] While we typically assume that there must be some original literal meaning behind an idiom, it is not clear that this is the case. Since the idiom is clearly well entrenched already in the Pyramid Texts, it is not clear that we should take the idiom literally, either in the Pyramid Texts or in later texts.

Conclusions

It is difficult enough for outsiders describing another living religion to convey an accurate understanding that religion's tenants to the satisfaction of adherents of that religion. It is much harder to do so for a dead religion as we have not the advantage of living adherents to correct our misconceptions. The only possible means we have of getting the tenets right is to examine the texts carefully.

From patterns and interpretations found in the texts one can construct an alternate theory of the parts of the human being and the various ways in which beings are related to each other. The *b3* is a general category of which the *rmṯ* 'man,' the *nṯr* 'god,' the *3ḫ* 'angel,' and the *mwt* 'demon, or damned' are specific entities. There is a consistent pattern of setting up a dualistic opposition of *b3* 'soul,' and *ḏ.t* or *ẖ3.t* 'body' beginning in the Pyramid Texts but flourishing from the Middle Kingdom on. The *k3* 'memory' or 'fate' is not related to the *b3* or the *3ḫ*, but is both the memory of the departed that remains behind them on earth and the fate they go to.

---

isb w3.t n=k k3=k ḥnʿ b3=k "go far away for yourself, your ka with your ba." P. Ryerson (Ptolemaic) in Allen, T.G., *The Egyptian Book of the Dead Documents in the Oriental Institute Museum at the University of Chicago* (= *OIP* 82), Chicago 1960, plate XXVII.

isy w3w n k3=k ḥnʿ b3=k 3ḫw ʿpr n sšm=sn "Go far away for your ka with your ba, an akh equipped for their guiding" pTurin 1791 (Late Ptolemaic), in Lepsius, *Totenbuch der Ägypter*, Tafel XXXIV.

170 Žabkar, *A Study of the Ba Concept in Ancient Egyptian Texts*, p. 137 n. 81.

171 Tomb of Herymeru architrave, line 3, in Hassan, *Mastabas of Princess Hemet-Rʿ and Others*, pp. 76-77, plate LVI; Strudwick, *Texts from the Pyramid Age*, p. 219.

172 Žabkar, *A Study of the Ba Concept in Ancient Egyptian Texts*, p. 51.

173 CT 344 IV 366; 821 VII 22; 936 VII 142.

174 CT 703 VI 335.

175 *Urk.* I 71; PT 475 § 948, 478 § 975, 512 § 1165; CT 297 IV 50, 343 IV 355, 344 IV 366, 556 VI 157, 703 VI 335, 712 VI 343, 753 VI 382, 821 VII 22, 936 VII 142; Schweitzer, *Das Wesen des Ka*, pp. 18, 50, 82; Žabkar, *Study of the Ba Concept in Ancient Egyptian Texts*, p. 7.

Between Identity and Agency in Ancient Egyptian Ritual*

Harold M. Hays

Represented in the hieroglyphs of Berlin stele 1204 is the first person account of the Middle Kingdom official Icherneferet,[1] detailing the thirty[2] steps he took while participating in rites for the god Osiris Foremost of the Westerners at the *bz.w št3* 'mysteries'[3] at Abydos. As this autobiographical slice-of-life dominates the greater part of the stele, there is no doubt as to the central message he wished to leave to posterity there:[4] in the construction of ritual equipment and images of deities, in instructing priests in their tasks, in arraying the divine Lord of Abydos in finery, and in carrying out rites for the god as a priest, this singularly capable individual had indeed done his duty.

But Icherneferet places his deeds in context by preceding his account with a letter from his king Senwosret III.[5] More precisely, it is an *wḏ-ni-sw.t*, a 'royal decree'[6] commanding that his subject go to Abydos 'to make (*iri*) a monument for my father Osiris Foremost of the Westerners, and to embellish (*smnḫ*) his mysteries'.[7] Icherneferet's first words after the frame[8] of the royal command demonstrate his full compliance with the king's instructions, through appropriation of the instrumental terms of the mission, *iri* and *smnḫ*:

* My many thanks to J.F. Borghouts, M. Conde Escribano, and L. Corcoran for comments on and corrections to an earlier version of this essay.

1 See Sethe, *Lesestücke*, pp. 70-71; Schäfer, H., *Die Mysterien des Osiris in Abydos unter König Sesostris III* (=*UGAÄ* 4), Leipzig 1904; and Simpson, W.K., *The Terrace of the Great God at Abydos: The Offering Chapels of Dynasties 12 and 13*, New Haven 1974, pl. 1; with translation at Lichtheim, M., *Ancient Egyptian Autobiographies Chiefly of the Middle Kingdom* (=*OBO* 84), Freiburg 1988, pp. 98-100.

2 About thirty, so long as one includes clauses where a first person pronoun subject is not expressed but may be read, such as at Sethe, *Lesestücke* 71, 5-6: *ms(=i) nṯr.w imiw-ḫt* 'me bearing the gods of the following'. Even if one does not, the difference between reading such forms thus or as passives is not substantial, because the account's intention is to list the events in which his involvement was instrumental. These many deeds may be more broadly grouped into four acts; see Assmann, J., *Tod und Jenseits im Alten Ägypten*, Munich 2001, pp. 310-312.

3 On which see Kucharek, A., 'Die Prozession des Osiris in Abydos. Zur Signifikanz archäologischer Quellen für die Rekonstruction eines zentralen Festrituals', in: Mylonopoulos, J. and Roeder, H. (eds.), *Archäologie und Ritual. Auf der Suche nach der rituellen Handlung in den antiken Kulturen Ägyptens und Griechenlands*, Vienna 2006, pp. 53-64; Lavier, M.-C., 'Les mystères d'Osiris à Abydos d'après les steles du Moyen Empire et du Nouvel empire', in: Schoske, S. (ed.), *Akten des vierten internationalen Ägyptologen Kongresses München 1985*, Band 3 (=*BSAK* 3), Hamburg 1989, pp. 289-295; and Assmann, *Tod und Jenseits*, pp. 308-312.

4 At his presumably *ex voto* chapel. See Simpson, *Terrace*, pp. 22-23, under ANOC 1, with reference to criticism at Lichtheim, *Ancient Egyptian Autobiographies*, p. 84.

5 Which in turn is contextualized by titularies of the king and other elements of the stele, including the separate and prominent display of Icherneferet's own titles and name; see the schematic representation of Hare, T., *ReMembering Osiris. Number, Gender, and the Word in Ancient Egyptian Representational Systems*, Stanford 1999, pp. 34-43.

6 For literature on *wḏ.w-ni-sw.t* 'royal commands', see Kloth, N., *Die (auto-) biographischen Inschriften des ägyptischen Alten Reiches. Untersuchungen zu Phraseologie und Entwicklung* (=*BSAK* 8), Hamburg 2002, p. 168 n. 592.

7 Sethe, *Lesestücke*, p. 70, 17: *r ir.t mn.w n it(=i) wsir ḫnti-imn.tiw r smnḫ bz.w=f št3*

8 For the sense of *frame* as active contextualization, as 'something we do', see Culler, J., *Framing the Sign. Criticism and Its Institutions*, Norman 1988, p. xiv.

> I acted (*iri*) in accordance with that which His Majesty commanded,
> embellishing (*smnḫ*) that which my lord had commanded for his father Osiris, Foremost of the Westerners, Lord of Abydos, resident in the Thinite nome.
> I performed (*iri*) the office of Son Beloved of Him for Osiris, Foremost of the Westerners:
> I embellished (*smnḫ*) his great bark of eternity and perpetuity.[9]

Though having done much on his own at Abydos for the god—in constructing, instructing, investing, and performing—Icherneferet had after all been ordered there. The stele he set up thus represents the intersection of his interests with those of the king and the god. Especially in this way, it has to do with the relationship between his individual activities and the most dominant structures of the world around him, namely the state and cult; it thus has to do with the notion of *agency*, with how an individual maintains, changes, or ignores the structures of the society within which he is embedded.

An agent within ritual may be said to be a person who performs a ritual action upon a ritual object.[10] Even more essentially, an agent is someone who does something, and the term *agency* refers most simply to the capacity and office of action. But in the humanities the terminology is regularly used in studies relating the individual to the collective in a quasi-technical fashion, albeit with widely varying connotations.[11] As invocation of the term *agency* orients a discussion upon how an individual interacts with his society (or with the *doxa* shaping his actions), it participates in the social science tension between 'holism' and 'individualism'.[12]

In Icherneferet's case, his act of agency involved the maintenance of the structures of his society: in performing cult, he participated in acts of central ancestral authority, doing the same kinds of things done by generations before him[13] at 'Abydos, the first ancient place of Neberdjer'.[14] And in acting for the king, he was neither subverting nor ignoring the structuration radiating from the monarch; he was adhering to it.

And yet—as ironic as it may seem given the thirty deeds of service detailed by him as implicit evidence of worthiness—Icherneferet's compliance with cult and king must have had the necessary consequence of suppressing his own identity during the act.

---

[9] Sethe, *Lesestücke*, p. 71, 2-4:
ir.k(w) mi wḏ.t.n ḥm=f
m smnḫ wḏ.t.n nb=i n it=f
wsir ḫnti-imn.tiw nb 3bḏw sḫm ˁ3 ḥr(i)-ib t3-wr iw
ir.n=i z3 mr=f n wsir ḫnti-imn.tiw
smnḫ.n=i wi3=f wr nḥḥ ḥnˁ ḏ.t

[10] Cf. the terminology's use at Lawson, E.T. and McCauley, R.N., *Rethinking Religion. Connecting Cognition and Culture*, Cambridge 1990, pp. 85-86 and similarly at McCauley, R.N. and Lawson, E.T., *Bringing Ritual to Mind. Psychological Foundations of Cultural Forms*, Cambridge 2002, esp. p. 23.

[11] See Dornan, J.L., 'Agency and Archaeology. Past, Present, and Future Directions', in: *Journal of Archaeological Method and Theory* 9 (2002), pp. 303-329, p. 304. The terminology's most influential employment is by Pierre Bourdieu and Anthony Giddens; see the summaries thereof at Dornan, *Journal of Archaeological Method and Theory* 9, pp. 305-308, and Krüger, O., Nijhawan, M. and Stavrianopoulou, E., '"Ritual" und "Agency". Legitimation und Reflexivität ritueller Handlungsmacht', *Forum Ritualdynamik* 14 (2005), http://www.ub.uni-heidelberg.de/archiv/5785, pp. 7-13.

[12] On the historical position of the term's technical usage in the social sciences in respect to these polarites, see Gillespie, S.D., 'Personhood, Agency, and Mortuary Ritual. A Case Study from the Ancient Maya', in: *Journal of Anthropological Archaeology* 20 (2001), pp. 73-112, pp. 73-75.

[13] According to Lichtheim, *Ancient Egyptian Autobiographies*, pp. 55-58, 85-88, and 129, the earliest dated stele attesting to the dramatic rituals is from year 9 of Senwosret I (Louvre C3), with the advent of the 'Abydos Formula' appearing already in Dynasty 11. On this formula, see further Lavier, M.-C., 'Les mystères d'Osiris', p. 210, and Wegner, J., *The Mortuary Complex of Senwosret III: A Study of Middle Kingdom State Activity and the Cult of Osiris at Abydos*, Ph.D. dissertation University of Pennsylvania 1996, pp. 62-69. It is conceivable that rites like those performed by Icherneferet had existed in some form since the Old Kingdom; see Griffiths, J.G., *The Origins of Osiris and His Cult*, Leiden 1980, p. 78.

[14] CT 60 I 255e (B10C): *3bḏw p3.t tpit n(i)t nb-r-ḏr*.

The Delegation of Agency

In sending a decree to a specific person, Senwosret III engaged himself in a practice already centuries old, when a letter from the king to one of his subjects could be expressed as an *wḏ-nỉ-sw.t* 'royal decree',[15] and in framing his stele's account with the content of that letter, Icherneferet was claiming the same kind of status-by-association already claimed centuries before him by others, who had likewise signaled to posterity their favor by inscribing letters from that most august personage:[16] here are two men, king and subject, both consciously positioning themselves within the traditions of their society. And though one might otherwise have imagined that the specific actions performed by Icherneferet were prompted by personal initiative—by his heart—his citing of the royal command as the first element of his text cedes initiative, planning, and motivation to his ruler. In view of Icherneferet's blatant embrace of tradition, I aver that he may be seen as an illustrative protagonist, an example of a type: a member of sacerdotal officialdom of a sort evident since the Old Kingdom, whence the simple and time-honored rule of obedience. Unquestionably the Egyptian priest was an agent in the rites he performed—in that he did and said things—but everything done was done under the aegis of the authority of command and command's authorization. One might more precisely call someone like Icherneferet an instrument of the state.[17]

State and religious duty are condensed in the person of the monarch. In Egyptian temples the king is ubiquitously[18] represented in relief making offerings to the gods, and he is portrayed just as ubiquitously in text making them to the dead in the formulaic phrase *ḥtp-ḏỉ-nỉ-sw.t* 'the offering which is given of the king'.[19] His service in temple and tomb is paired in a Middle Egyptian text often discussed by Jan Assmann, 'The King as Sun-priest', as it transparently expresses the ideological reach of the monarch's knowledge, powers, and responsibilities. One of those responsibilities is the performance of cult. As for the king, 'he gives offerings to the gods and mortuary offerings to the Akhs', the beatified dead:[20] in principle, it was the king who officiated in temple and tomb. Even for the 'Ritual of Amenophis',[21] where the royal name

---

[15] With 'the same term also used for more formal royal edicts', as observed by Wente, E.F., *Letters from Ancient Egypt*, Atlanta 1990, p. 17.

[16] The Old Kingdom letters of this kind have been republished and their connections to autobiographical texts discussed at Eichler, E., 'Zu den Königsbriefen des Alten Reiches', SAK 18 (1991), pp. 141-171.

[17] Contrast notions of agency where it is construed as revolving around subversion of established order, as with Mitchell, J., 'Ritual Structure and Ritual Agency. "Rebounding Violence" and Maltese *festa*', in: *Social Anthropology* 12 (2004), pp. 57-75. For the position that agency and the structures around the individual are inseparable, see Joyce, R.A. and Lopiparo, J., 'PostScript: Doing Agency in Archaeology', in: *Journal of Archaeological Method and Theory* 12 (2005), 365-374. For reference to the relationship between ritual and the maintenance or subversion of social structure, see below n. 93.

[18] Scenes of the High Priest of Amun Herihor offering to Theban gods at the temple of Khonsu constitute an obvious exception, but they are understood by Römer, M., *Gottes- und Priesterherrschaft in Ägypten am Ende des Neues Reiches* (=*Ägypten und Altes Testament* 21), Wiesbaden 1994, p. 25, to be in the tradition of statues of priests emplaced in the temple, 'wobei der prominente Anbringungsort der Darstellung an der Stelle des räuchernden Königs besonders günstig für die Erlangung göttlicher Gnade war', and thus the scenes stand 'in der Tradition der Priesters als Stellvertreter des Königs im Kult'.

[19] On the royal and cultic significance of the phrase, see Assmann, J., 'Totenkult, Totenglauben', *LÄ* VI, cols. 659-676, col. 663.

[20] See Assmann, *LÄ* VI, cols. 662-663. For the text, see Assmann, J., *Der König als Sonnenpriester. Ein kosmographischer Begleittext zur kultischen Sonnenhymnik in thebanischen Tempeln und Gräbern* (=*ADAIK* 7), Gluckstadt 1970, p. 19, and further exemplars at Karkowski, J., *Deir el-Bahri VI. The Temple of Hatshepsut. The Solar Complex*, Warsaw 2003, pp. 31, 180, and 205, with translations of the whole at Assmann, J., *Ägyptische Hymnen und Gebete*, 2nd ed., Freiburg 1999, pp. 97-99, and Parkinson, R.B., *Voices from Ancient Egypt*, Norman 1991, pp. 38-40. From the Luxor version B 9-10 + B 4-5: *ỉw=f ḏỉ<=f> ḥtp.t n nṯr.w pr.t-ḫrw n 3ḫ.w.*

[21] Or better, 'das Opferritual des Neuen Reiches', a term adapted from Arnold, D., *Wandrelief und Raumfunktion in ägyptischen Tempeln des Neuen Reiches* (=*MÄS* 2), Berlin 1962, p. 9, by Tacke, N., 'Das Opferritual des ägyptischen Neuen Reiches', in: Metzner-Nebelsick, C. (ed.), *Rituale in der Vorgeschichte, Antike und Gegenwart*, Rahden 2003, pp. 27-36, p. 31 with n. 28.

severally occurs in the position of ritualist,[22] Alan Gardiner draws out an important distinction between king as donor and those who actually performed the rites, because '...the real performers were priests, and their ranks are several times indicated'[23] in the paratext accompanying that ritual's recitations. The king's name is there on papyrus just as his name is on the temple wall:[24] it is an expression of the ideal, of what took place in theory.

In practice, as Gardiner said and as is very well known,[25] the role of officiant was performed by his subjects, as in our example case of Icherneferet. But from the Egyptian point of view it is not a question of pretending to be king;[26] the king does not command his subject to usurp 'royal prerogative'. It is a matter of royal delegation to perform particular actions and particular sacerdotal offices. Apropos Abydos, the stele of another Middle Kingdom official recounts that, 'His Majesty caused that I sacrifice cattle even in the temple of Osiris, Foremost of the Westerners in Abydos, Tawer'.[27] But the place might have been wherever any temple was. Already in the Old Kingdom, one finds the king appointing specific persons to priestly service (with attendant grants of land),[28] authorizing the establishment of teams of priests for the mortuary cult of his subjects,[29] and making provisions for the unhindered performance of cult.[30] Reaching forward in time, royal authorization is unequivocally expressed within the script to the daily rites performed for the god Amun-Re at Karnak, as given in the Dynasty Twenty-five Papyrus Berlin 3055:[31] 'I indeed am a *ḥm-nṯr*-priest', announces the priest reciting the liturgical script; 'it was the king who commanded me to see the god'.[32]

Seen from the point of view of delegation, Icherneferet's framing of his account not only singles him out as one worthy of regard by virtue of his association with the highest member of society, it also declares his very authorization for participating in rites in the first place. The command passes him the skeptron—the staff or scepter of office, the symbol of authorized

---

[22] On the mention by name of royal officiants within the 'Ritual of Amenophis', see Gardiner, A., *Hieratic Papyri in the British Museum. Third Series. Chester Beatty Gift*, London 1935, pp. 101-105.

[23] Gardiner, *Hieratic Papyri*, p. 104.

[24] Where the difference in media dramatically affects the representation of ritual. On walls as opposed to papyri, dynamics of self-presentation come into play, owing to the public nature of the medium.

[25] As noted, for example, at Assmann, J., 'Das Bild des Vaters im Alten Ägypten', in: Tellenbach, H. (ed.), *Das Vaterbild in Mythos und Geschichte*, Stuttgart 1976, pp. 12-49, p. 41, and see Assmann, J., 'Unio liturgica. Die kultische Einstimmung in götterweltlichen Lobpreis als Grundmotiv "esoterischer" Überlieferung im alten Ägypten', in: Kippenberg, H.G. and Stroumsa, G.G. (eds.), *Secrecy and Concealment. Studies in the History of Mediterranean and Near Eastern Religions* (=Numen Book Series 65), Leiden 1995, pp. 37-60, p. 49.

[26] Compare Frood, E., 'Ritual Function and Priestly Narrative. The Stelae of the High Priest of Osiris, Nebwawy', *JEA* 89 (2003), pp. 59-81, pp. 73-75 with n. 29, following Hare, *ReMembering*, pp. 39-40.

[27] Dyroff, K. and Pörtner, B., *Aegyptische Grabsteine und Denksteine aus süddeutschen Sammlungen*, Leipzig 1904, pp. 2-7 and pl. II (=Sethe, *Lesestücke*, p. 74, 19-20): *ḏỉ.n ḥm=f zft=ỉ ỉwꜣ.w m ḥw.t-nṯr n(ỉ)t wsỉr ḫntỉ-ỉmn.tỉw m tꜣ-wr ꜣbḏw.*

[28] See Urk I 26, 11 (see also 25, 4-6): *ỉn ḥm n(ỉ) wsr-kꜣ=f wḏ wꜥb n ḥw.t-ḥr nb.t rꜣ-ỉn.t* 'It was the Majesty of Userkaf who commanded the performance of priestly service for Hathor, mistress of Ra-inet'.

[29] See Goedicke, H., *Königliche Dokumente aus dem Alten Reich* (=*ÄgAbh* 14), Wiesbaden 1967, p. 209 fig. 27, 3-4 (see also 7-8) (= Urk I 302, 13-14; see also 302, 18–303, 1): *ỉw wḏ.n ḥm(=ỉ) ṯz.t n=k sḥḏ ḥm-kꜣ 12 r ḥw.t-kꜣ n(ỉ)t ḏ.t=k r wꜥb n=k r šd.t n=k ꜣbd* 'My Majesty has commanded the setting up for you of twelve Hem-Ka inspectors for your own Ka-house in order to perform priestly service for you and to recite for you the monthly service'.

[30] As at Goedicke, *Königliche Dokumente*, fig. 5 (= Urk I 213, 8-9; see also Urk I 212, 10-13): *ỉr.n ḥm(=ỉ) nw n(ỉ) ḫw.wt nỉw.tỉ ptn m-ꜥ ssr.w pn n-mr.wt wꜥb šd.t ꜣbd ỉr.t-ḫ.t-nṯr m nỉw.tỉ ptn* 'My Majesty has commanded this exemption of these two pyramid cities in this manner precisely in the interest of priestly service, recitation of the monthly ritual, and the performance of divine ritual in these pyramid cities'.

[31] On authority and authorization in this text, see further Gee, J., 'Prophets, Initiation and the Egyptian Temple', *JSSEA* 31 (2004), pp. 97-107, pp. 99-100.

[32] pBerlin 3055 IV, 2 (rite 9 of Moret, A., *Le rituel du culte divin journalier en Égypte d'après les papyrus de Berlin et les textes du temple de Séti Ier, à Abydos*, Paris 1902): *ỉw ḥm ỉnk ḥm-nṯr ỉn nỉ-sw.t wḏ wỉ r mꜣꜣ nṯr*. See also pBerlin 3055 IV, 6 (rite 11): *ḥr=ỉ zꜣ tw r nṯr ṯz pḫr nṯr.w ỉry n=ỉ wꜣ.t zn=ỉ ỉn nỉ-sw.t wḏ wỉ r mꜣꜣ nṯr* 'Sight of mine, shield yourself from the god (vice-versa). Gods, make a way for me that I may pass. It was the king who commanded me to see the god'.

speech—to adopt a metaphor of the sociologist Pierre Bourdieu[33]. It is a dogmatic or abstract precondition to the performance of the rites. Performed under such a precondition, the actions of the ritual cannot of themselves be efficacious[34]; the utterances recited for the god and the actions done for him are not of themselves *performative*:[35] their illocutionary force[36] is not inherent; the performance of cult by living priests demands the imprimatur of authority.

But from the moment of authorization on, the bestowed office was at times something like a piece of property, capable of being sold,[37] bequeathed in a testament to one's children,[38] or otherwise claimed by hereditary right.[39] So also could the authorization be transmitted on the spot by the delegate to his subordinates. Thus Icherneferet informs his reader that 'I set the temple personnel at their tasks, causing that they know the daily ritual[40] and the calendrical rituals':[41] the king's appointee ensured that the other ritualists knew the roles they were to fill in cult. This is not merely to be involved in a single ritual event, the mysteries proper, but to ensure that the officiants were trained in the regular operation of service throughout the course of each day, throughout the entire year. Through such direction, the delegation becomes a chain: from king to subaltern, and from subaltern to lieutenant.

Having authority over temple personnel and the actions they are to perform, it is also significant that our illustrious and illustrative protagonist is an outsider: Icherneferet was raised in the court of the king[42] and sent to Abydos to execute a royal command; this is control extended over the periphery from the center,[43] the imposition of a vision from a remote

---

[33] For the metaphor of the skeptron, see Bourdieu, P., *Language and Symbolic Power*, Thompson, J.B. (trans.), Cambridge 1991, p. 109.

[34] The point is that it is not enough that the ritual be performed, but that it must be performed by persons with certain qualifications. Cf. Tambiah, S.J., 'Form and Meaning of Magical Acts', in: Lambeck, M. (ed.), A *Reader in the Anthropology of Religion*, Oxford 2002, pp. 340-357, p. 352, where ritual and magical acts are asserted to be illocutionary or performative by virtue of being performed 'under the appropriate conditions'. See the second rule identified for performative utterances by Austin, J.L., *How to Do Things with Words*, 2nd edition, Cambridge 1962, p. 34 (see also pp. 15 and 53): 'The particular persons and circumstances in a given case must be appropriate for the invocation of the particular procedure invoked', and the extensive elaboration of Austin's observation at Bourdieu, *Language*, pp. 107-116.

[35] The term *performative sentence* 'indicates that the issuing of the utterance is the performing of an action' (Austin, *How to Do Things*, p. 6); i.e. such a statement not only says something but also accomplishes something: saying so makes it so. On how the notion of performativity has been applied to ritual in history of religions, see Penner, H.H., 'You Don't Read a Myth for Information', in: Frankenberry, N.K. (ed.), *Radical Interpretation in Religion*, Cambridge, 2002, pp. 153-170, pp. 156-158. The notion of performativity has seeped into Egyptology in respect to religion and ritual as at Assmann, J., *The Search for God in Ancient Egypt*, Lorton, D. (trans.), Ithaca 2001, p. 51, in respect to magical practice at Eschweiler, P., *Bildzauber im alten Ägypten* (=*OBO* 137), Freiburg 1994, p. 14, and in respect to grammar; see the summary thereof at Servajean, F., *Les formules des transformations du Livre des Morts* (=*BdE* 137), Cairo 2003, pp. 33-38.

[36] That is, what the words of a statement accomplish (illocution) as opposed to the true-false meaning they communicate (locution) or the affective consequences they inspire (perlocution); see Austin, *How to Do Things*, pp. 99-100.

[37] As occurs in the Ptolemaic pMarseille 299 recto; see Vittmann, G., 'Ein thebanischer Verpfründungsvertrag aus der Zeit Ptolemaios' III. Eurgetes. P. Marseille 298+299', *Enchoria* 10 (1980), pp. 127-139 and pls. 12-15.

[38] As at Urk I 26, 14-16 (also cited above): *ỉn ỉgr ms.w(=ỉ) ỉpn wꜥb ḥw.t-ḥr nb.t rꜣ-ỉn.t mr ỉrr(=ỉ) ḏs(=ỉ) sk w(ỉ) ḫp.k(ỉ) r ỉmn.t nfr(.t) m nb ỉmꜣḫ* 'Furthermore, it is these children of mine who are to perform priestly service for Hathor, mistress of Ra-inet as I now do myself, after I am passed to the perfect West as a possessor of veneration'.

[39] See for example the filio-paternal cliché of pBerlin 3055 X, 2 (= rite 25 of Moret, *Le rituel du culte*): *ỉw ḥm ỉnk ḥm-nṯr zꜣ ḥm-nṯr m rꜣ-pr pn* 'and indeed I am a *ḥm-nṯr*-priest, the son of a *ḥm-nṯr*-priest in this temple'.

[40] Lit. what pertains to the hand of every day, i.e. the daily action.

[41] Sethe, *Lesestücke*, p. 71, 6-7: *ḏi.n=ỉ [ỉmỉw]-wnw.t-ḥw.t-nṯr r ỉr(ỉ)wt=sn ḏi(=ỉ) rḫ=sn n(ỉ)t-ꜥ n(ỉ)t rꜥ nb ḥꜣb.w-tp-tr.w*. On *tp-tr.w* as seasonal festivals, see Spalinger, A., 'The Limitations of Formal Ancient Egyptian Religion', *JNES* 57 (1998), pp. 241-260, p. 242 with n. 11.

[42] Sethe, *Lesestücke* p. 70, 20-21: *ḏr nt(ỉ)t ỉn=k ỉs pw m sbꜣ.t(ỉ) ḥm=ỉ ỉw ḫpr.n=k ỉs m sḏ.t(ỉ) ḥm=ỉ sbꜣ.t(ỉ) wꜥ n(ỉ) ꜥḥ=ỉ* 'because it is the case that you were brought to be a pupil of My Majesty, and you became a protege of My Majesty, a singular student of my palace'.

[43] For a nuanced theoretical consideration of center versus periphery in respect to king, court, cult places, and cult, see Gundlach, R, 'Hof, Zentrum und Peripherie im Ägypten des 2. Jahrtausends v.Chr.', in: Gundlach, R. and

authority over the local conduct of ritual practice, and, through that, dogma. It is a fresh imposition of a new pattern of action, or it is an existing structure's maintenance and refinement.[44] Better said, the deeds of the agent, empowered by the monarch, contribute to the formulation or adjustment of the fundamental basis of ritual practice, influencing the practice and beliefs of other officiants there. Indeed, the royal control and protection of the cults has a long history, stretching back to Dynasty Five[45] and before.[46] And even in the construction of temples, as at Heliopolis under Senwosret I,[47] the king directs a member of his court[48] to go forth and execute the preliminary work for him.[49] Afterwards the king arrives to personally oversee the demarcation of the temple's foundations:

> The appearance of the king in the fillet of two plumes,
> with all the masses in his following:
> the chief lector priest, scribe of the god's book,
> stretching the cord and untying the line,
> when the putting into the earth was done in this temple.[50]

Abstractly establishing the ideological grounds for the hierarchical structuring of society,[51] the very space in which ritual is performed has its concrete design imposed from outside and above, along a chain of delegation suspended from the one ritualist whose identity genuinely mattered: the king.

The Place of the Non-royal Agent's Identity

In performing ritual for the god, Icherneferet does not act for himself; he acts for the king. And there are incentives for him to do so. The most obvious is the enhancement of his personal status through having been commanded to a sacred task and through having fulfilled it. That the task and accomplishment were significant to his status is evident in the record of these events commemorated in Berlin stele 1204. Here one sees the Egyptian personality advanced through

---

Klug, A. (eds.), *Das ägyptische Königtum im Spannungsfeld zwischen Innen- und Außenpolitik im 2. Jahrtausend v.Chr.*, Wiesbaden 2004, pp. 21-34.

[44] Compare the scope of the notion of 'redemptive hegemony' (how the practice of human activity can not only change a structure but also reproduce it) in Bell, C., *Ritual Theory, Ritual Practice*, Oxford 1992, pp. 81-88. See also below, n. 92.

[45] See Goedicke, *Königliche Dokumente,* fig. 2 (= Urk I 170, 11—172, 11) for the Dynasty Five decree of Neferirkare for the divine temple at Abydos.

[46] As with the representation of the foundation rite (presumably of a temple) involving the king and the goddess Seshat, dated to the reign of Kha'sekhemwi, for which see Engelbach, R., 'A Foundation Scene of the Second Dynasty', *JEA* 20 (1934), pp. 183-184, pl. 24.

[47] As narrated in the Berlin Leather Roll 3029, for the text of which see de Buck, A., 'The Building Inscription of the Berlin Leather Roll', in: *Studia Aegyptiaca* I, pp. 48-57; and on which see Piccato, A., 'The Berlin Leather Roll and the Egyptian Sense of History', *LingAeg* 5 (1997), pp. 137-159, pp. 137-142 with n. 1 for further references.

[48] In this case, like Icherneferet, the king's instrument is a *ḫtm.tỉ-bỉ.tỉ* and *ỉmỉ-r3 pr.wỉ nbw pr.wỉ ḥḏ* (Berlin 3029, II 7-8).

[49] Instructing him to *wḏ n ỉry.w r ỉr.t ḫft š3(=ỉ) n=k* 'make command to those who are to act according to my assignment to you' (Berlin 3029 II 13).

[50] Berlin 3029 II 13-15:
ḫʿ.t ni-sw.t m sšd šw.ty
rḫy.t nb.t m-ḫt=f
ḫri-ḥ3b.t ḥry-tp zš-mḏ3.t-nṯr
ḥr pḏ šs wḥʿ w3w3.yt
ḏi.w m t3 ỉr.w m ḥw.t tn

[51] Cf. cult centers shaping societies at Smith, J.Z., *To Take Place. Toward Theory in Ritual,* Chicago 1987, pp. 51-52.

royal service, just as in the Old Kingdom:[52] the privilege of the assignment presumably adds to his cultural capital, to the dimension of social status which is built out of non-material qualities. The stele commemorates and even creates that status, freezing it in time as a fixture of self-presentation. In maintaining the structure of his environment through adhering to royal command, the experience distinguishes the ritualist from among his peers.

Not only in the performance of divine cult does the Egyptian have incentives,[53] but also in the performance of rites for the dead: he secures their praise and protection in this world. Thus an official may say 'I am one praised of his father, mother, and lords in the necropolis, through performing mortuary service for them, performing their ceremonies on'[54] various feast dates. And the dead, for their part, are advised, 'Watch over your survivors, for they perform your ceremonies!'[55] As the living ritualist expects forceful protection from his ethereal benefactors, a descendant can make this sort of appeal in a Letter to the Dead from the First Intermediate Period:

> Your condition is absolutely like a living one
> by the command of the gods who are in the sky and earth.
> You will put an end to the enemies, evil of character,
> of[56] your house, of your brother, your mother, /// and her excellent son, Merer,
> for as you were *iqr*-excellent upon earth,
> so are you *mnḫ*-excellent in the necropolis,
> with mortuary service performed for you,
> the Haker-ceremony[57] performed for you,
> the Wag-ceremony[58] performed for you,
> and bread and beer given to you upon the table of Foremost of the Westerners,
> with a going downstream in the night-bark, a going upstream in the day-bark,
> and truth of voice given to you beside every god,
> as I make the praise of the dead for you![59]

---

[52] See Assmann, J., *Stein und Zeit. Mensch und Gesellschaft im alten Ägypten*, Munich 1991, pp. 187-189. For further references and for the asseveration of individuality in the Old Kingdom, see van Walsem, R., 'Diversification and Variation in Old Kingdom Funerary Iconography as the Expression of a Need for "Individuality"' in: S. Seidlmayer (ed.), *Acts of the Symposium Religion in Contexts: Imaginary Concepts and Social Reality in Pharaonic Egypt, Berlin 29-31 October 1998, Berlin (in press).*

[53] On the principle of reciprocal benefit from the gods as a result of loyal devotion to them through human action, see Assmann, J., 'Weisheit, Loyalismus und Frömmigkeit', in: Hornung, E. and Keel, O. (eds.), *Studien zu altägyptischen Lebenslehren*, Gottingen 1979, pp. 11-73, esp. pp. 28, 39, and 47.

[54] Urk I 217, 12-13: *ỉnk ḥzy n ỉt=f mw.t=f nb.w=f m ẖrỉt-nṯr m pr.t-ḫrw n=sn ỉr.t ḥꜣb=sn m* various festivals.

[55] PT 667 §§1942b-c (Nt): *stp zꜣ=k ḥr tpỉw=k tꜣ ỉr=sn ḥꜣb.w=k*

[56] Lit. against.

[57] On this ceremony, see Helck, W., 'Die Herkunft des abydenischen Osirisrituals', *ArOr* 20 (1952), pp. 72-85, pp. 78-79, and Assmann, J., *Altägyptische Totenliturgien. Band 2. Totenliturgien und Totensprüche in Grabinschriften des Neuen Reiches*, Heidelberg 2005, pp. 474-476, with n. 78 for further references.

[58] On this ceremony, see Assmann *Altägyptische Totenliturgien. Band 2*, pp. 303-304, with further references at p. 416 n. 106.

[59] Louvre E 6134, ll. 5-20 (see Piankoff, A. and Clère, J.J., 'A Letter to the Dead on a Bowl in the Louvre', *JEA* 20 [1934], pp. 157-169):
ỉw ḫr(ỉ)t=k mr ꜥnḫ ḥḥ n(ỉ) zp
m wḏ nṯr.w nt(ỉ)w m p.t tꜣ
ỉr=k ḏr n ḫft(ỉ)w ḏw.w qd
r pr=ṯn r sn=k r mw.t=k /// n zꜣ=s ỉqr mrr
ntk ỉqr tp tꜣ
ntk mnḫ m ẖrỉt-nṯr
pr.t(w)-ḫrw n=k (For the delay of *n=k* after *ḫrw* in this expression, cf. the text cited below n. 103)
ỉr.t(w) n=k hꜣkr
ỉr.t(w) n=k wꜣg
rḏỉ.t(w) n=k t ḥnq.t ḥr wḏḥw n(ỉ) ḫntỉ-ỉmn.tỉw
ḫd=k m msk.t(y)t ḫnt=k m mꜥnḏ.wt

The ritually cared-for dead exert themselves on this world for the material benefit of those who make ritual possible: just as the king receives direct benefits from the gods on earth[60] for his performances as *nb ỉr.t ẖ.t* 'lord of ritual', so do non-royal delegates expect to receive reciprocal reward for their observance of filial duties. 'But as for any lector priest or any Ka-servant who will act /// and speak for me at this tomb of mine of the necropolis, I will be their protector',[61] declares the dead. Even a purely spoken service yielded benefit both to its deceased recipient and its doer. As one Middle Kingdom stele substantiates its appeal to the living:

> because the breath of the mouth[62] is beneficial for the titled dead,
> and this is not something through which one wearies,
> and because it is more beneficial for the one who does it
> than for the one for whom it is done:
> it is the one who is helped who protects the one who is upon earth.[63]

Significantly, this same sentiment is repeated as social dogma in the 'Loyalist Instruction',[64] emerging in the Middle Kingdom[65] and transmitted in multiple copies in the New Kingdom. Further incentives for the maintenance of cult are encoded in other socially prescriptive texts. In the *Admonitions of an Egyptian Sage*, a Dynasty Nineteen papyrus the text of which dates back to as early as the Thirteenth,[66] the reader is told:

> Remember the chewing of natron
> and the preparation of white bread by a man on the day of washing the head.
> Remember to set up the flagstaffs and to carve the altar,
> with the W'ab-priest cleansing the cult places,
> with the temple painted like milk,
> and to make sweet the scent of the horizon[67] and to maintain offering-cakes.
> Remember to cleave to the ritual instructions and the arrangement of dates,
> and to remove one initiated into priestly service for being physically corrupt:
> that is to do it wrongly;
> that is to remove the heart of [a man] /// on the day before eternity,[68]

---

rḏi.t(w) n=k mꜣꜥ ḫrw r-gs nṯr nb
ỉr(=ỉ) n=k ḥz.w(t) n(ỉ) m(w)t (mwt).t

[60] Ubiquitous in the various formulaic statements placed in the mouths of gods on temple walls in scenes since the days of Djoser (see Kahl, J., Kloth, N. and Zimmermann, U., *Die Inschriften der 3. Dynastie* (=*ÄA* 56), Wiesbaden 1995, p. 116 [Ne/He/4]) and thereafter throughout pharaonic history.

[61] From the tomb of Khentika; see James, T.G.H., *The Mastaba of Khentika Called Ikhekhi* (=*ASE* 30), London 1953, pl. 5 B13-15: *ỉr swt ẖri-ḥꜣb.t nb ḥm.w-kꜣ nb ỉr.t(ỉ)=s /// ḏd n(=ỉ) ḥr ỉz(=ỉ) pn n(ỉ) ẖrit-nṯr ỉw(=ỉ) r wnn m ḥꜣy=sn.*

[62] The formula is identified by Vernus, P., 'La formule «le souffle de la bouche» au Moyen Empire', *RdE* 27 (1975), pp. 139-145.

[63] Berlin 7311, K 1-2 (Berl. Inschr. I, 180, corrected via collation with the photograph of Simpson, *Terrace*, pl. 32):
ḏr-nt(ỉ)t ṯꜣw n(ỉ) rꜣ ꜣḫ (sỉ) n sꜥḥ
nn nw m wrd.t ẖr=s
ḥr-nt(ỉ)t ꜣḫ (sỉ) n ỉrr
r ỉrr.w n=f
ỉn sm.w mkk ḥr(ỉ)-tꜣ

[64] See Posener, G., *L'Enseignement loyaliste: sagesse égyptienne du Moyen Empire* (Centre de recherches d'histoire et de philologie II. Hautes études orientales 5), Geneva 1976, §14.6-12. On this passage therein, see also Loprieno, A., 'Loyalistic Instructions', in: Loprieno, A. (ed.), *Ancient Egyptian Literature. History and Forms* (=*PdÄ* 10), Leiden 1996, pp. 403-414, pp. 411-412.

[65] On the stele of Sehetepibre (Cairo 20538), for which see Sethe, *Lesestücke*, pp. 68-69.

[66] See Parkinson, *Voices*, p. 60, concerning the date of the papyrus and the disputed date of the text.

[67] Sc. the shrine, as observed by Parkinson, *Voices*, p. 121 n. 1.

[68] pLeiden I 344, col. 11, ll. 2-5 (Enmarch, R., *The Dialogue of Ipuwer and the Lord of All*, Oxford 2005, pp. 46-47 and 78):

when months are cou[nted] and years are known.

Service is to be performed and performed correctly, lest one incur ultimate consequences. In the *Instructions for Merikare,* composed in the First Intermediate Period[69] or Dynasty Twelve[70] and still copied in the New Kingdom, one encounters the exhortations:

A man should do what is beneficial for his Ba:[71]
perform priestly service <at> the monthly ritual; receive the white sandals:
go into the cult place;[72] unveil the mysteries:[73]
enter the sanctuary; and eat bread in the temple.
Make the <altar> flourish, add to the provisions,
and increase the daily service,
for it is what is beneficial for the one who does it.
Strengthen your monument according to your power:
one day gives to eternity,
an hour improves the future,
and the god knows of the one who acts for him.[74]

The benefits of participation in cult point eventually to eternity; they are accrued after death.

The mortuary literature well attests to this principle. In the Coffin Texts, for example, justification for one's very presence in the afterworld is based upon such observances in life.[75] Take this striking parallel to the 'King as Sun-priest' mentioned above: 'It has been made that I be in this land because of what I did, as I have set up divine offerings for the gods and mortuary offerings for the Akhs'.[76] And after death, the Egyptian claims involvement in the sorts of rites

---

sḫꜣ.w wšꜥ ḥzmn
sspd t-ḥḏ in z(ỉ) hrw iwḥ tp
sḫꜣ.w sꜥḥꜥ sn.w<t> ẖt ꜥbꜣ
wꜥb ḥr twry.t rꜣ.w-pr
ḥw.t-nṯr sqḥꜣ.ti mi irt.t
snḏm sti ꜣḫ.t srwd pꜣ.wt
sḫꜣ.w nḏr tp-rd šbšb sw.w
šd.t bz m wꜥb.t r ẖz.t ẖ.t
ir.t st pw m nf
szwn ib pw n(ỉ) [z(ỉ)] /// hrw ḫnty nḥḥ (The traces do not appear to suit *sḫꜣ.w.*)
ꜣbd.w tn[w] rnp.wt rḫ<.ti>

[69] As at Helck, W., *Die Lehre für König Merikare,* 2nd ed., Wiesbaden 1988, p.1.

[70] As argued at Quack, J.F., *Studien zur Lehre für Merikare* (=*GOF* IV.23), Wiesbaden 1992, pp. 120-136.

[71] Following the segmentation of Helck, *Lehre für König Merikare,* p. 39.

[72] Lit. 'join the temple'; see Wb iii 378.9.

[73] For this phrase, see Wb v 119.8.

[74] pLeningrad 1116A, 64-67 (Helck, *Lehre für König Merikare,* VI 6-10, pp. 38-39; see Quack, *Studien zur Lehre,* pp. 38-41):
ir z(ỉ) ꜣḫ.t n bꜣ=f
wꜥb.t(ỉ) <m> ꜣbd šzp ḥḏ.ty
ẖnm rꜣ-pr kfꜣ {ḥr} sštꜣ.w
ꜥq ḥr ẖm wnm t m ḥw.t-nṯr
swꜣḏ <wḏḥ>.w sꜥꜣ ꜥq.w
im ḥꜣ.w ḥr mny.t
ꜣḫ.t pw n ir-sy
srwd mnw.w=k ḫft wsr=k
iw hrw wꜥ ḏi=f n nḥḥ
wnw.t smnḫ=s n m-ḫt
rḫ.n nṯr m irr.w n=f

[75] Cf. below at n. 115.

[76] CT 39 I 171a-b (B16C): *isk ir wnn=i m tꜣ pn n(ỉ) ꜥnḫ.w ḥr ir.t(=i) smn.n(=i) ḥtp(.t)-nṯr n nṯr.w pr.t-ḫrw n ꜣḫ.w*

he performed during life: 'N. has come, even that she may establish offerings in Abydos'.[77] In the process, he can even maintain the solar cycle:

> N. is the one who stops that twisted one,[78]
> the one who comes to burn your bark upon the Great Plateau,
> for N. knows them by their names,
> and they will not reach [your] bark
> while N. is in it,
> that is, N. the maker of offerings.[79]

But given the present line of inquiry, there is something remarkable about these statements from the mortuary literature: like the stele of Icherneferet, they all apply to specific persons. They are tied to a certain individual within the community of the dead. What makes this fact remarkable is that, insofar as cult is concerned, the identity of the non-royal Egyptian matters only so long as it is a question of him reaping benefits—and yet these benefits must accrue *outside* the context of ritual activity proper.

The Displacement of the Agent's Identity

In talking about what he did at Abydos, it is of paramount importance to Icherneferet that the reader know his name, know his titles, and know that *he* was the one who performed rites for the god Osiris. And in the spells copied for Egyptians to be taken with them to the tomb, they are designated by name as the *otherworldly* performers of rites or as the dead *recipients* of rites. But within collective ritual as performed by living persons, there is only one non-royal individual who genuinely matters, and that is the divine or deceased beneficiary.

By *collective ritual* I refer to temple ritual, mortuary ritual, opening of the mouth,[80] and other points of group ritual emergence, the evidence for which stretches from the pyramids to Greco-Roman times, as the layered traces of a cultural complex occupying a central place in ancient Egyptian society, reaching into every dimension of it. The rites are collective inasmuch as they were typically performed by more than one ritualist, and because in any event they always involved at least two persons, one of whom was the beneficiary.[81] This beneficiary, the object of sacerdotal action, may be presumed both to be and to indwell the physical image of the god in his sanctuary, in the case of temple cult. Or, in the case of rites for a deceased

[77] CT 1079 VII 349b (B3C): *i.n N. tn smn=s ḫ.t m 3bḏw.* One may presume that the statement is made metaphorically.

[78] For *nbḏ* as 'twisted', see Borghouts, J.F., *Book of the Dead [39]. From Shouting to Structure* (=*Studien zum Altägyptische Totenbuch* 10), Wiesbaden 2007, p. 42 with n. 323.

[79] CT 1099 VII 414c-415e (B1Bo):
in N. pn ḫsf nbḏ pi
iy ḥr nzr wi3=k ḥr wʿr.t wr.t
iw N. pn rḫ sn m rn.w=sn
n pḥ=sn wi3[=k]
sk N. pn im=f
N. pn ir ḥtp.wt

[80] The close relationship between temple ritual and mortuary ritual in rites, phraseology, and participant role structures is demonstrated at Hays, H.M., 'The Worshipper and the Worshipped in the Pyramid Texts', *SAK* 30 (2002), pp. 153-167.

[81] The other being the ritualist, of course. Collective ritual texts in the mortuary literature are distinguishable on the basis of the grammatical person from personal recitations, wherein the beneficiary is also himself the performer; see further Hays, H.M. and Schenck, W., 'Intersection of Ritual Space and Ritual Representation. Pyramid Texts in Eighteenth Dynasty Theban Tombs', in: Dorman, P.F. and Bryan, B.M. (eds.), *Sacred Space and Sacred Function in Ancient Thebes* (=*SAOC* 61), Chicago 2007, pp. 97-115, p. 97 with n. 3.

person, he (or his Ka) is represented through or manifest in a statue or false door in his cult chapel.[82]

In Icherneferet's instance, it was a matter of performing service for a god, Osiris. Undoubtedly some of the specific rites he describes were in their details unique to Abydos, the occasion of his personal involvement being a calendrical event or otherwise special. But that these activities shared structural features with other temple rituals—for example, with the Greco-Roman Hour Vigil,[83] and with the mortuary liturgies of the Coffin Texts[84]—is not a serious question, at least to me: that the rites were done for a god, an inert image whose breast Icherneferet adorned with lapis lazuli and other precious materials,[85] is enough to place the events within a well attested framework.

But the case of Icherneferet is merely the touchstone of this essay. The assertion is a general one: one of the characteristics of collective ritual is that there is only one non-royal individual who genuinely matters, and that is the beneficiary. For this reason, many of the rites performed for Ra-Harakhti at the temple of Seti I are virtually identical to those performed for Ptah in the same place,[86] and they in turn can match rites done for Amun-Re at Karnak[87]—except that in each case the name of the deity being propitiated is changed to make the rite appropriate specifically to him. The identity of the sacred beneficiary was critical in the temple liturgies. So also in texts for the mortuary cult. Whether they were to be recited for the king Wenis or for the official Rekhmire,[88] the name of the passive[89] and inert beneficiary is inserted to tailor the rite to apply to him alone. The single meaningful variable among the different exemplars of such texts is the identity of the one for whom ritual is performed.

But as for the rest of the words the ritualists say, as well as their gestures, they remain the same. What, then, of the officiant's relationship to the text? In adhering to a fixed script, he follows the institutionalized furrows of his society.[90] In reciting, his actions are shaped by the stamp of repetition: the rite's words have been and were being repeated by still other ritualists elsewhere and elsewhen. In repeating gestures, he recognizes and submits to the words of his

---

[82] In practices established during the Old Kingdom. See Wiebach-Koepke, S., 'False Door', in: Redford, D.B. (ed.), *The Oxford Encyclopedia of Ancient Egypt*, vol. I, Oxford 2001, pp. 498-501, p. 499, and Fitzenreiter, M., *Statue und Kult. Eine Studie der funerären Praxis an nichtköniglichen Grabanlagen der Residenz im Alten Reich*, vol. I, http://www2.rz.hu-berlin.de/nilus/net-publications/ibaes3, pp. 545-549.

[83] On the Hour Vigil, see Assmann, J., 'Stundenwachen', *LÄ* VI, cols. 104-106, Willems, H., *The Coffin of Heqata (Cairo JdE 36418)*, Leuven 1996, pp. 382-384, Cauville, S., *Le temple de Dendara. Les chapelles osiriennes. Commentaire* (=*BdE* 118), Cairo 1997, pp. 70-72, and Assmann, *Tod und Jenseits*, pp. 349-371.

[84] In detail, see Assmann, J., *Altägyptische Totenliturgien. Band 1. Totenliturgien in den Sargtexten des Mittleren Reiches*, Heidelberg 2002, and in summary see Taylor, J., *Death and the Afterlife in Ancient Egypt*, London 2001, p. 199.

[85] Sethe, *Lesestücke* p. 71, 8-10: *ỉw sḫkr.n=ỉ šnb.t nb 3bḏw m ḫsbd.w ḥnꜥ mfk3.wt ḏꜥm.w ꜥ3.t(ỉ)wt nb.t m ḫkr.w n(ỉ)w ḥꜥ.w nṯr* 'I adorned the breast of the Lord of Abydos with lapis-lazuli, and turquoise, and every kind of precious metal and precious stone, as an adornment of the flesh of the god'.

[86] It is easiest to see the matches between the rites for the cults of each of the gods there (Isis, Osiris, Amun, Ra-Harakhti, and Ptah) through examination of Mariette *Abydos. Description des fouilles. Tome premier. Ville antique. Temple de Séti*, Paris 1869, pp. 34-76.

[87] See Moret, *Le rituel du culte*, pp. 2-3.

[88] Compare, for example, the vocative in PT 25 §18c in the pyramid of Wenis to that of TT 100 (Davies, N. de G., *The Tomb of Rekh-mi-Rê at Thebes* [=*PMMA* 11], vol. II, New York 1943, pl. 78).

[89] To be sure, the beneficiary of a rite may be orally exhorted to action by the reciting ritualist, but the physical reality is otherwise: stone, metal, and dead flesh are inert. For the observation that mortuary liturgies of an offering situation characterize the beneficiary as active (in contrast to those of an embalming situation), see Assmann, J., 'Verklärung', *LÄ* VI, cols. 998-1006, col. 1001; as a general rule, mortuary texts characterize the deceased as passive, in contrast to hymns, where the addressed personage is active, as noted by Assmann, J., 'Verkünden und Verklären. Grundformen hymnischer Rede im Alten Ägypten', in: Loprieno, A. (ed.), *Ancient Egyptian Literature. History and Forms*, Leiden 1996, pp. 313-334, p. 324.

[90] Cf. Kelly, J.D. and Kaplan, M., 'History, Structure, and Ritual', in: *Annual Review of Anthropology* 19 (1990), pp. 119-150, p. 140: 'The special power in ritual acts, including their unique ability to encompass contestation, lies in the *lack* of independence asserted by a ritual participant, even while he or she makes assertions about authority'; see also Rappaport, R.A., *Ritual and Religion in the Making of Humanity*, Cambridge 1999, pp. 32-33.

community,[91] and he is involved in perpetuating them.[92] It is to maintain the ritual structure. It is also to let that structure exert whatever power it has to structure the structure of society.[93] Or rather, it is to be instrumental in it.

And yet, as to the officiant's specific identity, within the ritual itself it is of singular irrelevance. As Assmann has observed, the priest does not speak as NN.[94] We do not hear the names of Ichernеferet or Niankhkai; the ritualists are effectively anonymous, inasmuch as they are not designated as specific members of society. Their identities are not part of the script. Better said, the living ritualist's personal identity is displaced in favor of the mantle of sacerdotal title or the role of divine officiant. Naturally, he often refers to himself with the first person pronoun, but when the ritualist happens to apply a name to himself in the scripts, it is never his own human one. An excellent example comes from the forty-fourth rite of the ritual performed at the sanctuary of the god.[95] The priest announces to the divine beneficiary:

> Hail to you, Amun-Re, lord of the thrones of the two lands,
> I have come even with a message of my father Atum:
> my arms are upon you as Horus,
> my hands upon you as Thoth,
> and my fingers upon you as Anubis, foremost of the god's booth.
> I am a living priest (lit. living servant) of Re,
> I am a W'ab-priest,
> and I am pure,
> my purity being the purity of the gods.[96]

Putting his hands upon the image of the deity,[97] the officiant speaks of himself in the first person. As for his named identity, two things are important: that he is in the office of priest and that, at once,[98] he is Horus, Thoth, and Anubis. It is the same when officiants address their fellows or otherwise refer to them, as for example when one priest calls out to another, 'O

---

[91] See Tambiah, S.J., *A Performative Approach to Ritual* (=*Proceedings of the British Academy* 65), Oxford 1981, pp. 140-141, where it is observed that two of the objectives of ritual (when construed as an act of communication) are submission to constraint and subordination to a collective representation.

[92] Cf. Bourdieu, *Language*, p. 116.

[93] For a summary of anthropological perspectives on the relationship between ritual and the maintenance or subversion of social structures, see Kelly and Kaplan, *Annual Review of Anthropology* 19, pp. 139-141.

[94] See Assmann, 'Unio liturgica', pp. 46, 53, and 56.

[95] In view of the fact that the officiant is within the sanctuary while identifying himself as a *wꜥb*-priest, cf. Gee, *JSSEA* 31, p. 98, who claims that such priests did not enter the sanctuary. The present passage contradicts this assertion.

[96] pBerlin 3055 XXVI, 4-6 (rite 44 of Moret, *Le rituel du culte*):
ỉ.nḏ-ḥr=k ỉmn-rꜥ nb ns(.wt) tꜣ.wy
ỉỉ.n=ỉ m wp.t n(ỉt) ỉt(=ỉ) ỉ.tm
ꜥ.wy=ỉ ḥr=k m ḥr
ḏr(.tỉ)=ỉ ḥr=k m ḏḥw.ty
ḏbꜥ.w=ỉ <ḥ>r=k m ỉnp ḫntỉ zḥ-nṯr
ỉnk ḥm ꜥnḫ n(ỉ) rꜥ
ỉnk wꜥb
ỉw=ỉ wꜥb.kw
ꜥb<=ỉ> ꜥb nṯr.w

[97] Cf. Heiden, D., 'New Aspects of the Treatment of the Cult Statue in the Daily Temple', in: Hawass, Z. (ed.), *Egyptology at the Dawn of the Twenty-first Century*, vol. 2, Cairo 2003, pp. 308-315, p. 312, who claims without support that the non-royal priest did not touch the image of the god. The present passage and others contradict this assertion.

[98] Or it may be that more than a several priests recited these lines, with one saying he is Horus, another saying he is Thoth, and so on.

butcher, give the foreleg to the lector priest and the heart to the companion![99] And from a different rite of the sanctuary ritual:

> I have ascended to you
> with the Great One (sc. Atum) behind me
> and <my> purity before me:
> I have passed by Tefnut,
>
> even while Tefnut was purifying me,
> and indeed I am a priest, the son of a priest in this temple.[100]

The officiant is everywhere referred to by generic title and by the names of gods. As the words he recited would be used by other priests, earlier and later, there and elsewhere, so also would his divine roles be played by others. Like the gestures he made, the sacerdotal roles belonged to society beyond the individual. In this manner, for the time being the participant yields his uniqueness and shapes his actions according to prescribed patterns, acknowledging and perpetuating them. His act of agency is to maintain this structure of his society.

Having observed that the officiant's personal identity is displaced, one would like to speculate after some reason for it. The most obvious is that the focus of collective ritual is not on the priests involved, but on the passive beneficiary for whom the rites are performed. Excluding the identities of the sacerdotal officiants has the effect of keeping the object of the activity in central place. Within the context of the ritual itself, it is not about the individualities of the living participants, but strictly about the divine beings whom they serve.

A further impetus for the separation of the officiant from his identity could well be found in the nature of the physical space into which he enters, since it is conditioned by the sacredness of the passive beneficiary: in addition[101] to receiving the skeptron, a precondition to entering ritual space is purity.[102] This holds for rites for a god as for a dead man. Thus Mehuakhti promises protection for '[any] of my own Ka-servants who will perform mortuary service for me while in a state of purity, that their heart be strong in respect to it, just as they are pure at the temple of the great god'.[103] According to the classical, Durkheimian theory, outside of the cultic space the ritualists 'are profane; their condition must be changed'[104] through purifications which prepare

> the profane participant for the sacred act, by eliminating from his body the imperfections of his secular nature, cutting him off from the common life, and introducing him step by step into the sacred world of the gods.[105]

---

[99] Opening of the Mouth rite 24, I b (KV 17) (Otto, E., *Das ägyptische Mundöffnungsritual*, vol. I, Wiesbaden 1960): *ỉ mnḥ ḏỉ ḫpš n ẖrỉ-ḥꜣb.t [ḥꜣ].ty n smr*

[100] pBerlin 3055 X, 1 (rite 25 of Moret, *Le rituel du culte*):
pr.n=ỉ ḥr=k
wr m-ḫt=ỉ
ꜥb.w<=ỉ> ḥr-tp ꜥ.wỉ=ỉ
zn.n=ỉ ḥr tfnw.t
swꜥb {k} wỉ tfnw.t
ỉw ḥm ỉnk ḥm-nṯr zꜣ ḥm-nṯr m rꜣ-pr pn

[101] For an assertion that the efficacy of ritual is contingent upon a combination of interdependent conditions, see Bourdieu, *Language*, pp. 111, 113, and 115.

[102] Reflected in the stele of Icherneferet at Sethe, *Lesestücke,* p. 71, 11: *ỉnk wꜥb ꜥ.wỉ m sẖkr nṯr sm twr ḏbꜥ.w* 'I was one pure of hands in adorning the god, a Sem-priest cleansed of fingers'.

[103] Edel, E., 'Inschriften des Alten Reichs III. Die Stele des *Mḥw-ꜣḫtj* (Reisner G 2375)', *MIO* 1 (1953), pp. 327-336, p. 328: *ḥm-kꜣ [nb] ḏ.t(=ỉ) pr(.tỉ)=sn-ḫrw n(=ỉ) wꜥb.w r nḫt ỉb=sn r=s mr wꜥb=sn r ḥw.[t]-nṯr n(ỉ)t nṯr ꜥꜣ*

[104] Hubert, H. and Mauss, M., *Sacrifice. Its Nature and Function*, Chicago 1964 [1899], p. 20.

[105] Hubert and Mauss, *Sacrifice*, p. 22.

That notion finds resonance in the priest's asseveration that 'I am pure, and my purity is the purity of the gods'.[106] Explicitly, the priest's condition of purity matches the purity of the divine beings he serves; implicitly, the statement distinguishes his present from his former state. Just as he physically separates himself through purification from the human world outside cultic space, thereby acquiring a divine condition, so also does he leave behind his profane identity and assume the mantles of authorized priest and of god. His separation from his human self facilitates passage between the contraries[107] of the mundane world and the ritual space. The purification signifies 'sheer difference', to use the phraseology of the historian of religions J.Z. Smith.[108] Indeed, because the Egyptian sentient world could be understood as consisting of four parts—the gods, the blessed dead, the king, and humanity[109]—the existence of a living Horus Icherneferet, or a Thoth Niankhkai would constitute a transgression across opposing categories.[110] But, together with authorization and the solemn marking of the passage by the act of purification, the specifically human agent is absent, and the ritualist steps across the threshold.

The specifically human agent is absent out of necessity, out of the nature of the efficacious action: it is really the gods who act. Thus the deceased is exhorted: 'Do not be distant from the gods, as they perform this utterance for you which they perform for Re-Atum'.[111] The replacement of human with divine identity could be seen as an *unio liturgica*, the term adopted by Assmann[112] to describe what he sees as the principle at work; according to him, in addition to involving the donning of a divine role, this principle has to do with knowledge of sacred words (*sꜣḫ.w*, 'transfigurations'[113]), their recitation,[114] and ritual action, with the point of the union being the facilitation of the human officiant's future transition into the afterlife.[115] But that is later.[116] Within the rites themselves, the focus remains the beneficiary, and to facilitate *his* transfiguration, a god must speak and act. Thus one may perceive the priest as god reciting the efficacious, Akh-making words to the deceased king: 'hear this word which Horus said to his

[106] pBerlin 3055 I, 7 (rite 2 of Moret, *Le rituel du culte*): *i͗w=i͗ wꜥb.kw ꜥb.w=i͗ ꜥb.w nṯr.w*

[107] For the notion of passages between contraries as a dynamic of ritual, see Bourdieu, P., *Outline of a Theory of Practice*, Nice, R., (trans.), Cambridge 1977, pp. 120 and 124-130. See Bourdieu, *Language*, pp. 117-126, on solemn transgressions as marks of consecrated difference. The very act of purification would have the effect of reinforcing the boundaries between the categories of man and god.

[108] See Smith, J.Z., *To Take Place*, p. 108.

[109] See Baines, 'Society', p. 129.

[110] And thus even in describing the ritual, Icherneferet does not specify the divine roles he played, although his chief role is implicitly evident in saying *i͗w nḏ.n=i͗ wnn-nfr hrw pf n(i͗) ꜥḥꜣ ꜥꜣ sẖr.n=i͗ ḫft(i͗)w=f nb(.w) ḥr ṯz* [*w*] *n(i͗) ndy.t* 'I saved Wenennefer on that day of the great battle; I felled all of his opponents on the bank of the [district] of Nedit' (Sethe, *Lesestücke* p. 71, 17-18), by virtue of the use of the verb *nḏ* in connection with Osiris and his enemies; see for example CT 17 I 51b-52a (B1P): *i͗w sšm=f ꜥnḫ n nṯr.w pr.t-ḫrw n rꜥ m mꜣꜥ.t i͗w ḥr ḫnt(i͗) ꜥnḫ.w nḏ.n=f i͗t=f wsi͗r snḥm.n=f nmt.wt smꜣ.w i͗t=f wsi͗r* 'He guides life to the gods, and a mortuary offering to Re in truth. Horus Foremost of the Living has saved his father Osiris, having nullified the action of the one who slew his father Osiris'.

[111] PT 606 §§1693c-1694a (M): *m ḥr i͗r nṯr.w i͗r=sn n=k rꜣ pw i͗r.n=sn n rꜥ-tm*

[112] See further Assmann, 'Unio liturgica'; Assmann, *Search for God*, pp. 68 and 250 n. 33; and Assmann, *Tod und Jenseits*, pp. 504-517.

[113] The Egyptian term *sꜣḫ.w* being equated by Assmann, J., *LÄ* VI, col. 998, with the category of 'Verklärungen', or 'mortuary liturgies'; the association is derived from observations of Goyon, J.-C., 'Littérature funéraire tardive', in: *Textes et langages de l'Égypte pharaonique III* (=*BdE* 64), Cairo 1974, pp. 73-81, pp. 79-81.

[114] To be clear, it should be observed that the activity indicated in the word *sꜣḫ* 'to make into an Akh' is not exclusively oral. For instance, when oil is applied to the deity's image, the priest recites, *ḏi͗.n=i͗ <tw> m ḥꜣ.t i͗mn-rꜥ nb ns(.wt) tꜣ.wy snḏm=f ẖr=s sꜣḫ=f ẖr=s* 'I have put <you> even in the brow of Amun-Re, lord of the thrones of the two lands, that he be made sweet by it, that he be made an Akh by it' (pBerlin 3055 XXXIII, 2-3, rite 55 of Moret, *Le rituel du culte*; for the reading *tw*, see pBerlin 3053 XXVIII, 3); similarly with the Pyramid Text version of the rite for mortuary cult, PT 77 §52c.

[115] See Assmann, *Tod und Jenseits*, pp. 510-511 and 516: 'Ihnen opfert man auf Erden und knüpft dadurch schon zu Lebzeiten eine Beziehung, die dann nach dem Tode durch Aufnahme in den Kreis der Opferempfänger belohnt wird'.

[116] See above at n. 76.

father Osiris, that you be an Akh thereby, that you be great thereby'.[117] Priest as god, *sꜣẖ.w* as recitation, and purity find confluence in the archaic or archaizing[118] Hour Vigil:

> Recitation by the Two Kites, the Mourners:
> Ah, let me purify my mouth; let me chew natron!
> I have censed myself with incense and fire,
> thus pure, cleansed, censed
> with the natron which went forth from Nekheb, with the incense which went forth from Punt,
> that which is sweet of scent, that which went forth as the Eye of Horus.
> How pure is the *sꜣẖ* of Osiris Foremost of the Westerners among the gods, the Followers of Horus!
> How beautiful is the *sꜣẖ* of Osiris Foremost of the Westerners!
> How ceremonial is the *sꜣẖ* of Osiris Foremost of the Westerners![119]

The recitation by the kites is the recitation of priestesses as Isis and Nephthys.[120] As the priest's mouth and body are purified, so are his *sꜣẖ.w*; in that condition, with him *wꜥb twrỉ snṯr*, the god's *sꜣẖ.w* are *wꜥb nfr ḥꜣbỉ*. The quality of purity is necessary not only for the passage between contraries, but for the speech to be efficacious, for it to be 'performative'.

Finally, although the king may delegate his subjects to perform the office of priest, once within that sphere deities such as Anubis, Re,[121] Geb,[122] and Thoth can be said to direct the action. Thus the deceased is told: 'May you go forth at the voice of Anubis, that he as Thoth

---

[117] PT 734 §§2264a-b (N): *sḏm mdw pw ḏd.n ḥr n ỉt=f wsỉr ꜣḫ=k ỉm ꜥꜣ=k ỉm*. Gods are also specified as those who make one into an Akh at, e.g., PT 431 §§781a-b (Nut); PT 437 §795b (Re); PT 483 §1083a (Geb); PT 610 §§1712a-c (Horus) and §§1713b-c (Thoth and Anubis); PT 690 §2106a (Horus); CT 50 I 231h (Thoth); CT 74 I 312e (Thoth); CT 229 III 295d (Isis); CT 237 III 309c (Isis); CT 345 IV 375a (Thoth); CT 1068 VII 330a (those in the Netherworld).

[118] That the Hour Vigil is marked by archaic language is observed by Cauville, *Le temple de Dendara*, p. 70, for the statements made by the lamenters, with global parallels to Pyramid Texts drawn out already by Junker, H., *Die Stundenwachen in den Osirismysterien*, Vienna 1910, p. 23.

[119] Hour Vigil XIII (Edfu) 61-71 (Junker, *Stundenwachen*):
ḏd-mdw ỉn ḏr(ỉ).tỉ ḥꜣ.(t)ỉw
ỉ ꜥb=ỉ rꜣ=ỉ wšꜥ=ỉ zmn.w
kꜣp.n(=ỉ) wỉ m snṯr ḥr ẖ.t
wꜥb.kw(ỉ) twr.kw snṯr.kw
m zmn.w pr m nẖb m snṯr pr m pwn.t
nḏm sty pr m ỉr(.t) ḥr
wꜥb.w(ỉ) sꜣẖ n(ỉ) wsỉr ḫntỉ-ỉmn.tỉw m-ꜥb nṯr.w šms-ḥr
nfr.w(ỉ) sꜣẖ n(ỉ) wsỉr ḫntỉ-ỉmn.tỉw
ḥꜣb.w(ỉ) sꜣẖ n(ỉ) wsỉr ḫntỉ-ỉmn.tỉw

[120] See Münster, *Untersuchungen zur Göttin Isis*, p. 23, for the identification of the *ḏrỉ.ty* 'kites' as Isis and Nephthys, an identification the tradition for which reaches back to the Old Kingdom, as at PT 535 §1280b (P): *ỉ ḥꜣ.t ỉ ḏr.t ꜣs.t tỉ ḥnꜥ nb.t-ḥw.t* 'the wailing-bird comes: the mourning-kite comes, that is, Isis and Nephthys'. For the vocalization with *-ỉ-* (*-y*), see CT 1033 VII 269a: *zꜣ ḏry.t n(ỉ)t wsỉr* 'the son of the kite of Osiris'. For further references on the mourning goddesses, see Cauville, *Le temple de Dendara*, p. 70 n. 117.

[121] As at CT 45 I 199f-200a (B12C): *ỉw wḏ.n n=ỉ rꜥ rḏỉ n=k tp=k smn n=k ṯz=k sẖr [n=k] ḫft(ỉ)w=k ỉnk msṯw.ty=k tp(ỉ) tꜣ* 'Re has commanded me (sc. Horus) that your head be given to you, that your spine be made firm for you, and that your enemies be made to fall [for you], for I am your offspring who is upon earth' and CT 590 VI 210h-i (S2P): *ꜥpr.n ḥr ỉt=f wsỉr m nby.t zkr ḏs=f wḏ.n rꜥ ỉrr=f sw* 'Horus has equipped his father Osiris with the Nebyt-collar of Zokar himself: Re has commanded that he do it'.

[122] As at PT 477 §967a-c (N): *ỉ.n Ne. ẖr=k wsỉr ... ỉry n=k Ne. nw wḏ.n gbb ỉry=f n=k* 'To you has Neferkare come, O Osiris,... that Neferkare do for you this which Geb commanded that he do', and PT 373 §657a-d (M): *ḥ(w) n=k ỉt ꜣzẖ n=k bd.t ỉr n tp(ỉ)w-ꜣbd.w=k ỉm ỉr n tp(ỉ)w-smd.wt=k ỉm m wḏḏ.t ỉr.t n=k ỉn ỉt=k gbb* 'Let barley be threshed for you, emmer harvested for you, being done at your first of the month festivals thereby, being done at your first of the half-month festivals thereby, as that which was commanded to be done by your father Geb'. See also PT 357 §§583c and 590b; PT 364 §612a; PT 367 §634a; and PT 369 §640b.

make you an Akh... through this your Sakh which Anubis commanded',[123] while 'it is Thoth who got the lectors, those who recite it during the deeds'.[124] In letting his actions be structured by royal authorization, the human goes to his task, becoming pure and stepping by title and divine name into the formalized ritual space; there, he acts as god, and his mandate stems from the gods.

And yet the ceding of initiative and acceptance of authorization has the effect of empowering the ritualist outside of ritual proper. Prior to it, the authorization imparts authority, granting control over subordinates. Once the ritual is complete, he enjoys the secondary benefits of cultural capital, a claim for superhuman protection in life, and post-mortem advantages. Among such other experiences and results as the agential ritualist might enjoy, in wielding the authorized language of his society he helps perpetuate and support its structures. And so, just as the ritualist stands between the motion of his performance and the stasis of the tradition incarnate in his king, so does a monument like that of Icherneferet emanate a myth of human identity. Irony: it was generated within a society in which that identity was in ritual effaced.

[123] PT 437 §§796c-797b (P): *pr=k ḥr ẖrw ỉnp s3ẖ=f ṯw m ḏḥw.tỉ ... m s3ẖ=k pn wḏ.n ỉnp*
[124] CT 590 VI 210f-g (S2P): *ỉn ḏḥw.tỉ ỉn ẖrỉw-ḥ3b.t šdd.w sw m šm.wt*

Material Agency, Attribution and Experience of Agency in Ancient Egypt

The case of New Kingdom private temple statues

Annette Kjølby

Introduction

Studies of materiality and 'material agency' have become increasingly popular in archaeology and anthropology. The current paper is intended to contribute to this field, by discussing one aspect of ancient Egyptian materiality, namely the human involvement with private temple statues during the New Kingdom (1539-1075 BC).[1] The paper thus addresses non-Egyptologists and Egyptologists alike.

Egyptian statuary was involved in many different forms of object-human interaction, and consequently provides a good case for the study of material agency and object-human interaction.[2] In the following I shall start by a theoretical introduction to different aspects of 'material agency'. This is used as a basis for discussing the role played by the private statues in the distributed personhood and extended presence of the individual represented as well as for discussing agent/patient relationships involved in the creation, presence and use of New Kingdom private temple statues.

Materiality and Material Agency

I use the term materiality in the broadest sense, covering the way human beings and society are influenced and shaped by the material world, as well as the way people use objects and other material aspects in acting, interacting and being in the world.[3] It includes the way thoughts, mind and personhood are materially expressed and extended as well as the way thoughts, experience and agency are materially constituted or entrenched.[4]

---

[1] Kjølby, A., *New Kingdom Private Temple Statues: A Study of Agency, Decision-making and Materiality.* Part I-II (unpublished PhD-thesis), University of Copenhagen 2007. This includes a study of material agency as well as the decision making process involved in the creation of the statues and how this related to the structuration of Egyptian society. The dissertation includes a study and catalogue of the New Kingdom private statues from the Karnak Temple Complex.

[2] See also examples in Meskell, L., *Object Worlds in Ancient Egypt. Material Biographies Past and Present,* Oxford/New York 2004; Meskell, L., 'Divine Things', in: DeMarrais, E. *et al.* (eds.) *Rethinking Materiality. The Engagement of Mind with the Material World,* Cambridge 2004, pp. 249-259; Meskell, L., 'Objects in the Mirror Appear Closer Than They Are.', in: Miller, D. (ed.) *Materiality,* Durham/London 2005, pp. 51-71; Gell, A., *Art and Agency. An Anthropological Theory,* New York 1998, pp. 133ff.

[3] For various uses of the term materiality see conveniently Miller, D. (ed.), *Materiality,* Durham/London 2005; Meskell, L., *Archaeologies of Materiality.* Oxford/Malden 2005; DeMarrais, E. *et al* (eds.) *Rethinking Materiality. The Engagement of Mind with the Material World,* Cambridge 2004.

[4] The expression of ideas, beliefs and concepts in the material world is largely what DeMarrais has defined as materialization (cf. DeMarrais, E. *et al.,* 'Introduction', in: DeMarrais, E. *et al, Rethinking Materiality,* p. 1); the external extension of mind into the world has been studied from different angles by e.g. Gell, *Art and Agency* and

One way of approaching or visualizing the materiality of statue creation is to look at agent/patient relationships in human-material involvement, as suggested by Gell.[5] Gell's study of material agency and 'the anthropology of art' is based on the idea that agency can be defined in terms of such agent/patient relationships. This means that every agent is an agent in relation to a patient and vice versa. This concept of agency is thus:

> relational and context-dependent ... My car is a (potential) agent with respect to me as a 'patient' not in respect to itself, as a car. It is an agent only in so far as I am a patient, and it is a 'patient' (the counterpart of an agent) only in so far as I am an agent with respect to it.[6]

As stated by Gell:

> This considerably reduces the ontological havoc apparently caused by attributing agency freely to non-living things, such as cars. Cars are not human beings, but they act as agents, and suffer as patients 'in the (causal) vicinity' of human beings, such as their owners, vandals and so on.[7]

I find the framework of agent/patient relationships a useful tool for identifying and visualizing the interaction spheres between objects and human agents, and it is used in the final part of this article to identify human-material interaction or engagement during the creation, use and presence of private temple statues in the world of the Egyptians.

A study of agent/patient relationships does not, however, in itself illustrate the nature of the interactions. To address the nature of human-object interactions I consider different aspects of 'material agency' and material influences on the Egyptians, their decision-making and practices in terms of

a) 'attributed material agency',
b) 'experienced material agency',
c) 'material influence', and
d) the object world as part of (and constituting) the extended or distributed person, mind and agency of human beings.[8]

This allows us to distinguish on various levels between interactions recognized and intended by the people who commissioned and produced a given object, and material influences, caused by human dwelling in a material world.[9]

Clark, A., *Being There. Putting Brain, Body and World Together Again.* Cambridge, Mass./London 1997; the role of material culture in the creation of new concepts and symbols and in enculturation is the focus of Renfrew's material engagement theory (Renfrew, C. 'Towards a Theory of Material Engagement', in: DeMarrais *et al.* (eds.), *Rethinking Materiality*, pp. 23-31; DeMarrais *et al.*, 'Introduction' in: DeMarrais *et al.* (eds.), *Rethinking Materiality*, p. 1).

[5] Gell, *Art and Agency*.

[6] Gell, *Art and Agency*, pp. 21-22.

[7] Gell, *Art and Agency*, p. 22.

[8] This includes what Gell defines as secondary agency. Gell distinguishes between 'primary' agents, i.e. entities endowed with the capacity to initiate actions or events through will or intentions, and 'secondary' agents, i.e. entities not endowed with will or intention by themselves but essential to the formation, appearance, or manifestation of intentional actions (notably Gell, *Art and Agency*, p. 36). Statues as well as other objects naturally fall into the second category.

[9] Also *Kjølby, Temple Statues* I.

Attributed vs. Experienced Material Agency

In some social interactions objects appear or participate as agents on a par with human beings. Thus:

> The immediate 'other' in a social relationship does not have to be another 'human being' ... Social agency can be exercised relative to 'things' and social agency can be exercised by 'things' (and also animals).[10]

Gell's definition of material agency is founded in the fact that people *attribute* intentions and awareness to objects and that an event is *believed* to happen because of an 'intention' lodged in a person or thing initiating a causal sequence:

> ... agency can inhere in graven images, not to mention motor cars. ... in practice, people do attribute intentions and awareness to objects like cars and images of the gods. The idea of agency is a culturally prescribed framework for thinking about causation, when what happens is (in some vague sense) supposed to be intended in advance by some person-agent or thing-agent. Whenever an event is believed to happen because of an 'intention' lodged in the person or thing which initiates the causal sequence, that is an instance of 'agency'.[11]

While agreeing that the 'other' in a social relationship can be a 'thing', I find this definition of agency problematic since it ties agency to intentionality. Following the definition offered by Giddens I use the concept of agency to apply to: 'events of which an individual is the perpetrator', and 'whatever happened would not have happened if that individual had not intervened'. Agency, thus, refers not to 'the intentions people have in doing things but to their capability of doing those things in the first place (which is why agency implies power)'.[12] Transferring this to the agency of 'thing'-agents it is necessary to distinguish between the aspects of material agency listed above. Consequently I discuss the 'intentionality' in material agency in terms of attributed and experienced material agency respectively.

I use the term *attributed material agency* for three purposes. First, I use it to describe the situation in which a person interacting with an object would be in a position to reason that the agency or intentionality of the object was not 'real', but attributed to it. This would for instance count for the relation between little girls and their dolls or a driver blaming his car for breaking down.[13] Secondly, attributed material agency may refer to an object-person interaction as viewed by outsiders, such as our analytical view on material agency experienced by members of other

---

[10] Gell, *Art and Agency*, p. 17-18.

[11] Gell, *Art and Agency*, p. 17.

[12] Giddens, A. *The Constitution of Society. Outline of the Theory of Structuration*, Cambridge 1984, pp. 9ff.; Giddens's definition of agency relates to human agents only, in that he adds that 'the individual [who is the perpetrator of the event] could at any phase in a given sequence of conduct have acted differently'. However, this is not the key point in this understanding of agency, rather the important part is that agency is tied to the capability of doing things rather than to intentionality. I may intend to do one thing, but by my action be the perpetrator (and thus the agent) of other unintended and/or unforeseen events. The approach thus stresses the analytical difference between the agents' capability to act, the motivations and intentions of the individual agents, and the consequences of their actions. For the use of the structuration theory of Anthony Giddens in relation to the creation of the private temple statues see Kjølby, A. 'Decision Making and Structuration: A Study of the Thoughts behind the Private Statues in New Kingdom Egyptian Temples', in: Jessen, M.D., Johannsen, N.N. and Jensen, H.J. (eds.), *Excavating the Mind: Cross-sections through Culture, Cognition and Materiality*, Århus, forthcoming (2009); Kjølby, *Temple Statues* I; Kjølby, A., 'Decision Making Processes: A Cognitive Study of Private Statues in New Kingdom Temples', in: Goyon, J.-Cl. and Cardin, C. (eds.) *Proceedings of the Ninth International Congress of Egyptologists* (=*OLA* 150), Leuven 2007, pp. 991-1000.

[13] Cf. the examples in Gell, *Art and Agency*, pp. 18-19.

cultures. Finally, on a cognitive level, it is possible to discuss strategies or mechanisms of *agency attribution* to or animation of non-living things such as cars, dolls, or Egyptian private statues, as I return to below.

Experienced material agency on the contrary, in my use of the term, refers to the insider's genuine experience of material agency. The term refers to the situation where the person interacting with an object would reason that the agency and intentionality of the object was real. I also use the term when the agency experienced is that of a force or being materialized or embodied in the object, as would for instance have been the case, when the Egyptians interacted with the individuals materialized in the private statues.

The terms attributed and experienced material agency thus refer to the perception or experience of a given person-object interaction as well as to mechanisms of agency attribution.

Material Influence, Distributed Personhood and the Extended Mind

The concepts of material influence, distributed personhood and extended mind on the contrary refer not to how a person-object interaction is perceived, but to how objects and other parts of the material world influence the experience, mind, and agency of people, either by their nature and presence in the world of human beings or by their role in the extension and distribution of mind, personhood, agency, and intentionality through space and time (i.e. how the material world is used by humans in thinking and interacting with other people and their world).

By *material influence* I refer to the influences that objects inflict on human experience, mind and agency as a result of our living and dwelling in a material world. This could be the physical properties of materials used for statue production, the impact made by already existing statues and other visual and written media or the practical experience with specific tools, etc.

The concepts of *distributed (or extended) personhood* and *extended mind* are inspired by works aiming at overcoming the mind-body-world boundaries, particularly the already cited work of Alfred Gell and the work of philosopher Andy Clark.[14]

The first aspect, which is the object of Gell's study, concerns the distributed or extended personhood, mind and agency of specific individuals or groups through time and space and is based on the view that,

> as social persons we are present, not just in our singular bodies, but in everything in our surroundings which bears witness to our existence, our attributes, and our agency.[15]

Thus:

> a person and a person's mind are not confined to particular spatio-temporal coordinates, but consists of a spread of biographical events and memories of events, and a dispersed category of material objects, traces and leavings, which can be attributed to a person and which, in aggregate, testify to agency and patienthood during a biographical career which may, indeed, prolong itself long after biographical death. The person is thus understood as the sum total of the indexes which testify, in life and subsequently, to the biographical existence of this or that individual.[16]

---

[14] Gell, *Art and Agency*; Clark, *Being There*; Clark, A. and Chalmers, D., 'The Extended Mind', in: *Analysis* 58(1) (1998), pp. 7-19; for study of personhood see also Fowler, C. *The Archaeology of Personhood. An Anthropological Approach*. London and New York 2004.

[15] Gell, *Art and Agency*, p. 103.

[16] Ibid., pp. 222-223.

As agents individuals or groups are thus not just where their bodies are 'but in many different places (and times) simultaneously'.[17] Applying this to Egyptian private temple statues, the statues should be seen not simply as images of the individuals represented, but as (detached) parts of their distributed person, i.e. personhood distributed or extended in the milieu, beyond the body-boundary. The concept of distributed personhood and agency is particularly relevant for the study of ancient Egyptian images and monuments, as the Egyptians themselves realized the potential of objects and monuments in distributing personhood and extending presence and agency through time and space, as I return to below.

Whereas the concept of distributed personhood and agency concerns the extension and distribution of personhood and agency through time and space beyond the body and lifetime 'barrier', the term *extended mind* is used mainly for explaining how the object (or material) world is used in thinking, and thus how the material world shapes us and expands our minds, for instance in the use of address-books, time-managers, computers, sketches, guide-lines, models, etc. but also through handling objects. The material world is thus recognized as an active element in thinking processes, an aspect touched upon by Gell,[18] but much more elaborately discussed by Clark.[19] According to this view, the mind is not just inside our body but extended outside our body through the use of the material world, which elaborates our memory, ability to process data, think creatively etc.

The use of monuments and objects in the construction of memory and distribution of personhood (or an individual) through time and space is not foreign to the study of ancient Egypt but has been dealt with in the work of Jan Assmann.[20]

New Kingdom Private Temple Statues - distributed personhood, attribution and experience of agency

Egyptian New Kingdom private statues were generally made to ensure the eternal well-being of the individual represented by preserving his name, his physical manifestation and ability to receive offerings and being remembered amongst and interact with the living. It established or negotiated his identity and person, by presenting him in words and image as a specific type of person (male/female, social and religious position/state). In the temples the few private statues found in their original placement indicate that the statues were generally placed in the more accessible areas by the pylons or in the courtyards, i.e. along the processional route taken by the participants in temple festivals and passed by the priests performing the offering cult for the gods. In comparison with the statues placed in private tomb complexes the placement in a temple complex provided the person represented with closeness to the gods and the king and to the offerings brought forth and activities taking place in the temple. It furthermore provided the owner with a more protected location and interaction with the 'priests and passers-by'. Finally it provided a good basis for negotiating the identity of the person represented as well as of the donor or patron who may be the 'statue owner' himself, a relative or the king.[21] The current

---

[17] Gell, *Art and Agency,* pp. 21. See further pp. 96ff.

[18] Ibid., pp. 221ff (most notably p. 236). Gell's use of the term is, however, blurred and it seems to largely overlap with his use of distributed personhood and distributed object, the latter being the index of distributed personhood and extended mind. On p. 236 he does, however, relate this to the view that '"thinking" takes place outside us, as well as inside us', which is the core of the idea of the extended mind.

[19] Clark, *Being There.*

[20] E.g. Assmann, J., *Stein und Zeit. Mensch und Gesellschaft im alten Ägypten,* München 1991; Assmann, J., *Death and Salvation in Ancient Egypt,* New York/London 2005 (abridged and updated version of Assmann, J., *Tod und Jenseits im alten Ägypten,* München 2001, translated by David Lorton).

[21] For a study of New Kingdom private temple statues including a catalogue of the New Kingdom private statues from the Karnak Temple Complex see Kjølby, *Temple Statues* I-II. For a study of the private temple statues of the Old and Middle Kingdoms see Verbovsek, A., *'Als Gunsterweis des Königs in den Tempel gegeben...'. Private Tempelstatuen des Alten und Mittleren Reiches.* (= *ÄAT* 63), Wiesbaden 2004.

section deals with the nature of private temple statues and how they were used to distribute the person of the 'statue owner' and extend his presence and ability to interact with the living as well as with the perception of this interaction.

To the ancient Egyptians statues materialized the essence and presence of the individual depicted. The identity and person of the statue owner were thus distributed or extended through time and place by the choice of motif and inclusion of his name, titles and in some cases biographical data on the statues.

The importance of the preservation of the name is clearly expressed in the standard phrase of private dedication texts 'it is his son [or another individual] who makes his name live' (*jn s3.f sꜥnḫ rn.f*), as well as in the wish for the name of the owner to endure in the temple expressed in some offering formulas.[22]

While the personal identity of an individual was preserved by the preservation of his name, his social persona or social identity was established and preserved through other means. The desire to establish and preserve one's social identity is thus conspicuously reflected in the consequent listing of titles, as well as in the genealogical and biographical information frequently written on the statues, and in the choice of motif.[23]

A person could be destroyed or erased by the destruction of his name and other earthly manifestations. Thus we see in Egypt examples of *damnatio memoriae*,[24] and monuments, including private statues, were frequently usurped or 'recycled' in later times. The wish to avoid oblivion could be expressed in curses on monuments, as exemplified by one Karnak statue from the very end of the New Kingdom, when the future king Herihor wrote on his scribe statue:

> As for any person who may remove this statue from its place after the course of many years, he shall be in the power of Amen, Mut, and Khonsu, and his name shall not exist in the land of Egypt; he shall die of hunger and thirst.[25]

Besides recording and thus distributing and preserving the awareness of his person, the statue provided the owner with a 'body' or manifestation amongst the living, by which he could interact with them and obtain the benefits of such interaction and thus extended his presence beyond his real body boundary.

The exact nature of images is debated. Images were often defined as *twt* (*twtw*),[26] the meaning of which may be found in its relation to the similar word *twt* meaning '(be) like'.[27] Schulz in a survey of Egyptian statue-terminology suggested that the term generally should be

---

[22] E.g. Scott, G.D., *Ancient Egyptian Art at Yale*, New Haven 1986, pp. 78, 128-131 (no. 73); Lipinska, J., *Deir el-Bahari IV. The Temple of Tuthmosis III. Statuary and Votive Monuments*, Warsaw 1984, pp. 25-26 (F636 (+ F706)).

[23] Kjølby, *Temple Statues* I-II. For the negotiation of social and religious identity through the choice of motif in the private temple statues in Karnak see Kjølby, *Temple Statues* I, pp. 132ff.

[24] Most clearly expressed by the erasure of kings from monuments and the Egyptian kinglists, particularly the cases of the Amarna Kings and Hatshepsut (see Brunner-Traut, E., 'Namenstilgung', *LÄ* IV, col. 338-341). The monuments of Hatshepsut's official Senenmut suffered some deliberate destruction of his name, although this was not consistent (for a discussion of the various damages to the monuments of Senenmut and their relation to the persecution of Senenmut, Atenist iconoclasm, natural damage and later persecution of pagan images see Dorman, P., *The Monuments of Senenmut. Problems in Historical Methodology*, London/New York 1988, pp. 144ff).

[25] *KRI* VI, 843-844 (§36.1). Translation in Scott, G.D., *The History and Development of the Ancient Egyptian Scribe Statue,* I-IV, (PhD dissertation, Yale University, New Haven), Ann Arbor 1989, p. 483.

[26] See discussion in Schulz, R., *Die Entwicklung und Bedeutung des kuboiden Statuentypus. Eine Untersuchung zu den sogenannten 'Wurfelhockern'*, I-II (= *HÄB* 33-34), Hildesheim 1992, pp. 700ff, which also includes other words for statue; also Hornung, E., 'Der Mensch als "Bild Gottes" in Ägypten', in: Loretz, O., *Die Gottebenbildlichkeit des Menschen,* München 1967, pp. 123-156.

[27] Here translated cf. Gardiner, H., *Egyptian Grammar. Being an Introduction to the Study of Hieroglyphs* (3rd edition, reprint 1988), Oxford 1957, p. 599; Schulz uses the German translation 'ähnlich sein, gleichen'.

understood as 'Abbild' i.e. an 'image' and thus as the 'wiedergabe eines Vorbildes, aber nicht als das Vorbild selbst'.[28] Assmann, however, suggested that:

> the statue [of a deity] is not the image of the deity's body, but the body itself. It does not represent his form but rather gives him form. The deity takes form in the statue, just as in a sacred animal or a natural phenomenon,[29]

and this is the position followed here for the relation between a person and his private statues as well.

The terms chosen for the making of a statue surely indicate that the image was perceived as a life-extender, a physical manifestation of a living being, hosting or giving form to such a being. Thus one term for sculptor was *sꜥnḫ* 'one who makes life', and the process of statue creation was defined by the term *msj* 'to bear' or 'give birth'; i.e. to 'form' or 'fashion' a statue.[30]

In order to understand the function and character of the statues it is necessary to consider Egyptian concepts of personhood. Persons to the Egyptians consisted of multiple constituent elements, which in life seems to have been united in the living individual, but in death 'emerged in its various aspects or constituent elements, which now took on a life of their own'.[31] These aspects of the person included the concepts of the *ba, ka, akh,* heart, shadow and name of the person as well as the body, the corpse and the mummy. A detailed description of the various elements is not necessary here.[32] Important in the present context is that humans (the deceased) could take on multiple manifestations.

One type of manifestation was the images of the person. Noteworthy in this regard is the inscription in the shrine of the mortuary chapel of Amenemhet (reign of Thutmose III), listing Amenemhet's stele on equal terms with other manifestations. We read:

> [Bringing all manner of good things].... in all his places .... [for the steward of the vizier,] Amenemhet, for his ka, for his stele belonging to this tomb which is in the Necropolis, for his destiny, for his life, for his place of origin, for his upbringing, and for his Khnum', and elsewhere in the shrine '[Bringing all manner of good things ..... for the scribe reckoner of the grain in] the granary of divine offerings of [Amun], Amenemhet, for his ka, for his stele ... for his [soul], for his illumination, for his corpse, for his shadow, and for all his modes of being (*ḫprw*).[33]

[28] Schulz, *Entwicklung*, p. 701: 'Auch über den speziellen rundplastischen Rahmen hinaus kann er als "Abbild" im weitesten Sinne verstanden werden und damit als wiedergabe eines Vorbildes, aber nicht als das Vorbild Selbst, auf bildlicher oder schriftlicher Ebene'.

[29] Assmann, J., *The Search for God in Ancient Egypt*, New York 2001 (Revised edition of Assmann, J., *Ägypten. Theologie und Frömigkeit eine frühen Hochkultur*, Stuttgart/Berlin/Köln/Mainz 1984, translated by David Lorton), p. 46; Assmann, *Theologie und Frömigkeit*, p. 57.

[30] *Wb.* II, p. 138, 12.

[31] Assmann, *Death and Salvation*, p. 87.

[32] The exact nature of the various elements is debated. See e.g. conveniently Gee this volume; Assmann, *Death and Salvation*, p. 89ff; Baines, J., 'Society, Morality, and Religious Practice', in: Shafer, B.E. (ed.) *Religion in Ancient Egypt. Gods, Myths, and Personal Practice,* Ithaca and London 1991, p. 145; Friedmann, F.D., 'Akh', in: Redford, D.B. (ed.) *The Oxford Encyclopedia of Ancient Egypt* I, New York 2001, pp. 47-48; Bolshakov, A.O., 'Ka', in: Redford (ed.), *Oxford Encyclopedia* II, pp. 215-217; Allen, J.P., 'Ba', in: Redford (ed.), *Oxford Encyclopedia* I, pp. 161-162.

[33] *Urk.* IV, 1060,9-1061,6. Translation in Davies, N. de G. and Gardiner, A.H., *The Tomb of Amenemhet (no. 82)* (= *The Theban Tomb Series* 1), London 1915, p. 99; alternative translation in Blumenthal *et al., Urkunden der 18. Dynastie. Übersetzung zu den Heften 5-6,* Berlin 1984, p. 416; Gee this volume.

Although the inscription does not mention Amenemhet's statues, and the inclusion of the stele on a par with other manifestations in the manner seen here is quite unique, it does exemplify the New Kingdom Egyptian belief in a person's multiple manifestations.

Formulations in mortuary texts from the New Kingdom and later clearly associate the statues of a deceased with other manifestations. For instance we read that:

> Your *ba* endures in the sky, your corpse is in the netherworld, your statues in the temples.[34]

While the deceased was present in the sky in his manifestation of *ba* and in the netherworld in his manifestation of corpse, he was present on earth in his statue-manifestations. An important aspect of New Kingdom Egyptian mortuary belief was the ability to 'go forth by day' and participate in the realm of the living in any form one wishes.[35] This wish is also expressed on the Karnak statue of Wensu, which in the offering formula asks Thoth and Anubis to

> grant coming forth upon the earth in order to see the sun disk, whether [being] a *ba* of heaven or a corpse of the netherworld.[36]

According to Gell, there are two basic cognitive strategies or mechanisms for attributing agency to non-living things and conceptually converting these into 'quasi-persons in artefact form'. One mechanism, defined as the *internal* strategy or theory of agency attribution, consists of:

> 'providing [an object] with a homunculus [i.e. inner person or mind], or space for a homunculus, or turning it into a homunculus within some larger entity'.[37]

I shall not take up a discussion of the usefulness of the concept of homunculi in general. The *internal* strategy is for instance the mechanism used in the animation of idols by conceiving them as containers of an inner person or mind (or soul, spirit etc.) or themselves as the mind by placing them within a container.[38]

The mechanism of conceiving an object as a 'container' of a mind is mirrored in the Egyptian idea of the *ba* of a god or of a deceased descending on or uniting with his image.[39] The Egyptian notion of the relation between the *ba* and the image was, however, not as dualistic as implied by the 'container' image. The *ba* was not conceived of as an inner mind of the image, but as a 'soul' descending on or uniting with the image. It was believed that the *ba* aspect of the deceased animated the statues and could also assume all other forms, a mechanism which is generally explained in Egyptological literature in terms of the German word *Einwohnung*, which may be translated by 'installation' or 'indwelling'. The concept originated in the mortuary belief and is expressed in statements from the 18th Dynasty, such as:

> May my *ba* alight on my images (*ꜥẖmw*) in the monuments I have made.[40]

---

[34] S. Sauneron, *Rituel de l'Embaumement*, Cairo 1952, 7,18. This and similar examples are given in Assmann *Death and Salvation*, p. 91 incl. note 16.

[35] Assmann, *Death and Salvation*, pp. 209ff.

[36] Cairo CG 42132 (JE 38373), lower left base; Translation in Scott, *History and Development*, p. 977.

[37] Gell, *Art and Agency*, p. 133.

[38] Ibid., pp. 126ff.

[39] Assmann, *Death and Salvation*, p. 215; Assmann, *The Search for God*, pp. 40ff; Lorton, D., 'The Theology of Cult Statues in Ancient Egypt', in: Dick, M. B. (ed.), *Born in Heaven Made on Earth. The Making of the Cult Image in the Ancient Near East*, Winona Lake, Indiana 1999, p. 152.

[40] *Urk.* IV, 1526,11-15. Translation in Assmann, *The Search for God*, p. 43.

In their aspect of *ba* the deceased could thus come forth from the realms of the beyond to enter their tombs and manifestations, participate in festivals and receive their mortuary meals as stated in several tomb inscriptions and offering spells,[41] and nicely summarized in one New Kingdom tomb, in which the owner asks:

> May my *ba* emerge, at the sound of its mortuary priest, to receive the offerings that has been brought to it.[42]

The efficacy of statues was brought about by the ritual generally described as 'the opening of the mouth' which transformed the created 'statue object' into a capable body materializing the person represented and ready to be animated by his *ba*. In the case of statues, the procedure was performed in the workshop and involved priests as well as the sculptor and the painter.[43] The 'opening of the mouth' ceremony could, however, be performed on any material manifestation of a person, whether a statue, a two-dimensional image or a mummy,[44] thus stressing the conceptual relation between these various manifestations. In this regard it is worth noticing that the word *ḏt*, which is usually translated as 'body', in fact referred to representation as well as body, thus erasing the distinction between the two.[45] This similarity is also expressed in the determinative used for words like mummy, corpse, body, statue, picture, form, etc.[46]

Private statues were thus conceived of as one of multiple manifestations of a person. Serving as a body and a materialization of his personal and social identity a statue was an essential part of the distributed person of an individual, extending his presence in the world of the living beyond his own physical boundary and beyond death. In this material form the person manifested in a temple statue could participate in the activities of the temple and interact with the living in a temple context. In such interactions his statue functioned as a recognized social other in the world of the Egyptians, permitting physical interaction between the living and the (animated) statue.

This leads us to the other cognitive mechanism or strategy of agency attribution; the *externalist* approach, by which an object is made into a (social) agent by 'stipulating for it a role as a social other'.[47] This mechanism is surely well-known from Egypt. Thus on a simple 'cultic' level priests in the temples would in the daily temple ritual treat the cult statues of the gods as real social others by waking, anointing, clothing and feeding them, thus carrying out the activities that one would carry out on behalf of a real body.[48] This elaborate process was most likely not performed for the private temple statues, which would simply have offerings presented before them or have their offering formula recited by the priests and passers-by, as it is expressed in

---

[41] See e.g. Assmann, *Death and Salvation*, pp. 330ff, 215ff.

[42] TT 277: Vandier d'Abbadie, J., *Deux Tombes ramessides à Gournet-Mourrai*, Cairo 1954, p. 430 (762), translation in Assmann, *Death and Salvation*, p. 330.

[43] For statues the full title of the ritual is 'Performing the opening of the Mouth in the Workshop for the Statue (*twt*) of N' (Otto, E., *Das Ägyptische Mundöffnungsritual* II (= *ÄA* 3), Wiesbaden 1960, 2.34; Lorton, 'Theology of Cult Statues', p. 147). For a detailed description see Otto, *Ägyptische Mundöffnungsritual*; H.W. Fischer-Elfert, *Die Vision von der Statue im Stein. Studien zum altägyptischen Mundöffnungsritual,* Heidelberg 1998; Lorton, 'Theology of Cult Statues', pp. 147ff; Assmann, *Death and Salvation*, pp. 310ff. For comparative studies see Gell, *Art and Agency*; Meskell, *Object Worlds*.

[44] It started as a ritual for bringing the tomb statue to life, but developed into a consecration ritual carried out on all sacred objects from offering stands to entire temples, e.g. Assmann, *Death and Salvation*, p. 312.

[45] Assmann, *Death and Salvation*, p. 106; also Assmann, *Tod und Jenseits*, p. 145.

[46] Gardiner, *Egyptian Grammar*, p. 447 (A53- A55).

[47] Gell, *Art and Agency*, p. 126ff, quotes p. 133.

[48] The details of the daily temple rituals need not be repeated here. See conveniently Lorton, 'Theology of Cult Statues', pp. 131ff; Gell also uses the daily temple ritual in illustrating the externalist strategy (Gell, *Art and Agency*, pp. 133ff).

the appeal to the living on some of the statues.[49] Thus for instance on a cuboid statue of Amenhotep son of Hepu during the reign of Amenhotep III we read the following appeal:

> O dignitaries of the King, prophets, *wa'b*-priests, lectors, noblemen and citiz[ens] – who shall pass by my statue, the King will love you, your Lord will be gracious, and you will favour all the gods of your cities, (if) you say 'a boon which the king gives....'.[50]

However, the presenting of offerings to the deceased or ancestral spirits, present in their this-worldly manifestations, is comparable to the more elaborate daily temple ritual.

The interaction with the dead or ancestral spirits in the offering services at the tombs was accompanied by the recitation of spells, which generally contained the following elements: An invitation to the deceased to ready himself to receive the offerings; formulas for presenting the offerings; 'sacramental explanation' of the offering, mentioning further actions of the deceased that result from receiving the offerings; and sometimes also a 'concluding text' in which the officiant speaks of himself and his activities on behalf of the deceased.[51]

The first part of the spell was meant to ensure that the deceased came forth from the realm of the dead by appearing in his tomb and animating his statue or 'being clad in your body' as it is formulated in some older spells.[52] The 'body' presumably referred to a 'cultic body' that the deceased put on and had disposal of in order to receive the offerings presented to him, namely the statue or the false door in the tomb.[53] The sacramental explanation connected the cultic sphere of human-deceased interaction (i.e. presenting offerings and recitation of spells) with the mythic sphere. While on a simple level the offerings would provide the deceased with nourishment, the sacramental explanation of the offerings meant that through the receiving of offerings the deceased became part of the sphere of the gods and transfigured ancestral spirits and it thus served as a medium for his salvation from the realm of death.

While a person's capacity to animate his statues and other monuments as a *ba* was essential for his ability to receive offerings, the offering formulas written on statues and other monuments ask specifically for offerings 'to the *ka* of' the owner.[54] Also a mortuary priest was called a *ka*-servant (*ḥm-k3*) in line with the priests of the gods who were called 'god's servant' (*ḥm-nṯr*), thus underlining that although the statue was animated by the descent of the *ba,* the presenting of offerings was equally or even more important in relation to the sustenance of the *ka.*

The connection between the *ba* and *ka* aspects of a person is nicely illustrated by the inscription on the Karnak statue of the mayor of Thebes, Sennufer, and his wife, Sentnay, which asks for:

> An offering which the king gives to Osiris, ruler of eternity and to the gods who are in the necropolis and to the door-keepers of the portals of the netherworld, that they may grant emergence as a living soul [*ba*] at the words of the summoner at the presentation of offerings to the ka of the mayor, Sennufer.[55]

---

[49] E.g. *Urk.* IV, 412; 1826; 1832-1833; 1835; 2175-2176. For a full list of appeals to the living on the New Kingdom private statues from Karnak see Kjølby, *Temple Statues* II, pp. 331-333 (table 5.4).

[50] *Urk.* IV,1826,7-13. Translation in Davies, B., *Egyptian Historical Records of the Later Eighteenth Dynasty* V, Warminster 1994, pp. 19-20. 'A boon which the king gives' is the *ḥtp dj nsw*(*t*).

[51] Largely citing Assmann, *Death and Salvation,* p. 331; for the provisioning of the dead and the offering service in the cult place of the tomb see Assmann, *Death and Salvation,* pp. 330ff.

[52] *Pyr.* §1300c [537]; 2119 [690]; translation in Assmann, *Death and Salvation,* p. 342.

[53] Assmann, *Death and Salvation,* p. 342.

[54] Besides the name and identity of the owner, the offering formula is the most common inscription on the temple statues, either in the form of the *ḥtp dj nsw*(*t*) formula ('A boon which the king gives...'), the *prrt nbt* formula or in a few cases just starting with the sentence *n k3 n* ('to the ka of') (Kjølby, *Temple Statues* II).

[55] *Urk.* IV, 1435,14-16. Translation in Cumming, B., *Egyptian Historical Records of the Later Eighteenth Dynasty* II-III, Warminster 1984, p. 134.

The *ka* concept is not agreed upon by modern scholars, and it is not the aim of the present work to develop this understanding. In the words of Assmann:

> (the *ka*) was the vehicle of the vindication that restored the individual's status as a social person, which had been destroyed by death. In other words the *ba* belonged to the physical sphere of the deceased, restoring his movement and his ability to take on form, while the *ka* belonged to his social sphere and restored his status, honor, and dignity.[56]

The presenting or recitation of offerings for statue owners in a temple context as well as the recitation of spells in the offering cult at the tomb reveals the statue or tomb owners as recipients of the attention given to them by the priests or passers-by i.e. as patients in an agent/patient relationship, which was intended to ensure the immortality of the statue owner. However, the Egyptians also attributed the person manifested in the statue a more active role as an agentive social actor, as indicated by appeals to the living on some statues.[57]

The agentive abilities of private statues (or the person present in the statue) become particularly clear when during the New Kingdom a few statue owners took a further step in their wish to obtain provisioning. In return for the presenting of offerings, pouring of libation or recitation of the offering formula they offered their assistance as intermediaries between the living and the god of a specific temple, thus doing favours for the people approaching the temple by taking their pleas to the god.

Thus on one of the statues of Amenhotep son of Hepu from the 10th pylon at Karnak the following proclamation was inscribed:

> O Upper and Lower Egypt, and every eye that shall see the sun-disk, those who come downstream and upstream to Thebes, in order to make supplication to the Lord of the Gods. Come to me, so that I may make a report of what is said to (me) to Amun in the Temple of Karnak. Make for (me) 'a boon which the King gives', and pour for me a libation from what is with you. I am a herald whom the King provides, in order to hear the words of the humble man, and in order that the affairs of the Two Lands may be brought forward.[58]

The deceased could be active in the sphere of the gods on behalf of the living, and in the same way as a prominent person could in real life transmit the petitions of the people to the king, he could in his afterlife transmit their petitions to the god (Amun). Although only very few statues have preserved an appeal to the living and even fewer state their role as intermediary between the living and the gods, the occurrence of intermediary statues reveals how the dead were perceived as real social others and active participants in the world of the living.[59]

---

[56] Assmann, *Death and Salvation*, p. 97; for an alternative interpretation of the phrase *n k3 n* ('to the ka of') see conveniently Gee this volume.

[57] E.g. *Urk.* IV, 412; 1826; 1832-1833; 1835; 2175-2176. For a full list of appeals to the living on the New Kingdom private statues from Karnak see Kjølby, *Temple Statues* II, pp. 331-333 (table 5.4).

[58] *Urk.* IV, 1833,11-18. Translation in Davies, *Egyptian Historical Records* V, p. 22.

[59] Only 3 of the 177 New Kingdom Private temple statues from Karnak states an intermediary function (= *Urk* IV, 1833 (no. 663), 1834 (no. 664), 1922 (no. 714)) all dating to the reign of Amenhotep III (Kjølby, *Temple Statues* II, pp. 331-333 (table 5.4)). A few temple statues from Deir el-Bahri specifically addresses women and promises to bring their requests to Hathor (Clère, *Les chauves d'Hathor* (=*OLA* 63), Leuven 1995, pp. 148-149 (BM41645) and 204-5 (BM1459)). For examples of interference of the dead in the life of the living, other than those mentioned here, see conveniently Baines, 'Society and Moral', pp. 147ff. The agentive abilities of the dead are most vividly expressed in 'letters to the dead', in which the writer addresses a deceased relative to change some unwanted circumstance or course of events. See conveniently Wente, E., *Letters from Ancient Egypt.* (= Society of Biblical Literature. Writings from the Ancient World 1), Atlanta 1990, pp. 210ff; also Gardiner, A.H. and Sethe, K., *Egyptian Letters to the Dead, Mainly from the Old and Middle Kingdoms*, London 1928.

From an analytic point of view the described interaction between men and statue(owner)s would be categorized as attributed agency. To the Egyptians the interaction with the statue was, however, experienced as real interaction with the person present in the statue. If confronted with their actions by an outsider, they would most likely not have reasoned that the interaction with the statue (or the person manifested) was only symbolic.[60] In the statues the barrier between subject and object was thus blurred.[61] The statue was a materialization of its owner, his mind, person and identity. The owner was present, he lived on the food presented to him or the offerings invoked by recitation, and had the potential to act for (or against) the living. The potency of the statue could be ruined by destroying its appearance, and with it the existence of the person materialized in the statue. The statue (as well as his other materializations) thus served as a distribution of his personhood, distributing or extending his person in time and space and thereby ensuring his immortality and ability to interact with the living.

Material Agency and Agent/Patient Relationships

During the production, presence and use of private temple statues, the statues participated in various agent/patient relationships, some of which have already been considered above. I shall now consider the interactions between the statue and the prototype or person represented, as well as between the statue and other living human beings.[62] These interactions are illustrated in Fig. 1, which is inspired by Gell's study of 'the art nexus' including relations between art objects, their makers (artists), prototypes and recipients.[63] Since the statue functioned as a medium in the relations between the other participants in these statue interactions, the interactions may be seen in terms of complex agent/patient relationships, in which the statue functioned simultaneously as agent and patient in relation to other participants.

I start with the interactions in which the statue from an analytical point of view can be defined as acting as a patient (P) in relation to priests and passers-by and as an agent (A) in relation to the statue owner, which may be summarized as follows:

Priests and passers-by (A) -> statue (P/A) -> statue owner (prototype) (P)

The main purpose of these interactions was to provide the person represented with various benefits. A statue ensured that the statue owner was provided for. This was accomplished either through the direct receiving of offerings, through the very presence of the statue in the temple near the offerings of the god, or invoked by the recitation of the offering formula by the passers-by.

The relevance of receiving offerings is clearly documented by the statue inscriptions, which usually include the offering formula (*ḥtp dj nswt*), which may at times be supplemented by a wish to receive the offerings that 'come forth' from the offering table(s) of specific gods (the *prrt nbt* formula). Some statues furthermore had the appeal to the passers-by asking them to

---

[60] For a similar view concerning the interaction with deities see Assmann, *The Search for God*, p. 47; for symbolic vs. idolatrous practices in the interaction with Egyptian gods see Gell, *Art and Agency*, p. 135.

[61] For the collapse of boundaries of subject and object see also Meskell, 'Objects in the Mirror', p. 57; Meskell, 'Divine Things', p. 253; and generally for discussion of the materiality and material agency of Egyptian statues see Meskell, *Object Worlds*; Meskell, 'Divine Things'; Meskell, 'Objects in the Mirror'; Gell, *Art and Agency*, p. 133ff.

[62] Similar relations can be identified for the agent/patient relationships of raw materials in relation to statues, artists and recipients, see Kjølby, *Temple Statues* I, pp. 219-221.

[63] Gell, *Art and Agency*, pp. 21ff, and particularly pp. 28ff; for critiques of Gell see e.g. Layton, 'Art and Agency: A Reassessment', *The Journal of the Royal Anthropological Institute* 9/3 (2003), pp. 447-464; Meskell, *Object Worlds*.

PATIENT \ AGENT	**Artist**	**Statue** (Index)	**Prototype** (Mental image or statue owner)	**Recipient** (Patron, priests, passers-by)
Artist	//// ////	- The quality of the statue influences the esteem and 'payment' / reward of the artist.	- The character of the *owner* is mediated by the artist. - The appearance of the *mental image* of an elite Egyptian, etc. is imitated by the artist.	- The patron commissions the statue -> and thus causes the artist's action
Statue (Index)	- The artist intentionally models and gives finish to the statue. - The artist's technical and artistic skills affect the quality and reception of the statue.	///// ////	- *The owner* is the cause of the form taken by the statue (by his/her gender, social status, position, etc.) - *The mental images* of an elite Egyptian and other concepts dictate the form taken by the statue.	*The patron* - Causes the statue to be made and decides the motif, material, etc. *The people interacting with the statues* - Offer food or recitation before the statue. - In some cases use the statue to mediate their petition to the god.
Prototype (Mental image or statue owner)	- The artists' knowledge of how to render the image correctly maintains the mental image of an elite Egyptian, etc. and works on behalf of the person represented.	- The statue functions as a manifestation of the owner. -Ensures his eternal life and extends his presence and memory in the world of the living, and in the temples near the king or god. - Ensures his ability to interact with the living, participate in cultic activity / procession in the temple. - Immortalizes his name, identity, etc. - Serves in the negotiation of identity. - Influences the well-being and existence of the owner in the afterlife. - Maintains or changes various mental images.	//// ////	*The patron* - Causes the immortality and provisioning of the owner. - Decides how he should be remembered, and thus negotiates his identity. - Contributes to the maintenance of the mental image of an elite Egyptian, male, female, etc. *The priests / passers-by* - Recall and remember the owner and effectuate his provisioning -> ensuring the owner's successful post-mortal existence.
Recipient (Patron, priests	- The artist's technical and artistic skills affect the recipients' reception of the statue.	- The statue induces the memory of the owner upon the living in the temple, and causes their interaction with the owner. - As a manifestation of the owner, the statue can do favours for the people approaching the temple.	Via the image: - The *person depicted* interacts in the life of the recipient. - *Mental images* (elite Egyptian, male / female, etc.) are reproduced in the mind of the recipient.	-*The patron* influences the spectators (negotiating identity, causing their memory of and interaction with the person/statue, etc.) - *The people seeing, hearing about and interacting with* the statue bring about the intentions of the patron

Fig. 1. Statue interaction.

recite the offering formula, as mentioned above. The agent/patient relationship between the statue and the person materialized in the statue was thus effectuated by the interaction between the statue, acting as patient, and the priests and passers-by, who presented offerings to the statue, carried offerings to and from the table of the gods, or recited the offering formula before the statue.

In addition to ensuring provisioning, the statues served the equally important purpose of bringing about the recollection of the person materialized, thereby contributing to his distributed person and stretching the memory of his identity and social persona in place and time. Such a purpose is for instance indicated by the passage in the above-mentioned dedication formula *jn* NN *sꜥnḫ rn.f*, in which the donor states to have given the statue in order to let the name of the receiver live.

The statue also influenced the priests and passers-by and may thus be seen not only as a patient but also as an agent in relation to these:

Statue (A) -> priests and passers-by (P)

In the examples just given it should therefore be added that the statue was not only a *patient* in relation to the priests and passers-by, in the sense that it was the 'receiver' of their offerings, remembrance, etc., but also an *agent* in relation to these, as it was the very presence of the statue in the world of these individuals that induced upon them the memory of and the need to effectuate provisioning for the person manifested. In other words its presence influenced the priests and passers-by and served as a memory device, extending their minds.

Another intended agentive role of some statues is expressed by the above-mentioned 'intermediary statues', where the statue owners offer their assistance as intermediaries between the living and a god of the temple. As an agent, the statue-manifestation caused the living to remember and provision for the owner and assisted the people approaching the temple by taking their petitions to the god.

To the relations between statues and the priests and passers-by we must add another agent/patient relationship in the involvement between people and statues, namely that between the patron and the other participants:

Patron (A) -> statue (P/A) -> living human beings and person manifested (P)

The outlined relations, between the statue and the person manifested (the 'statue owner') and between the statue and living human beings, were in fact largely the intended effect of the agency of the patron, who could be identical with the owner, a relative of the owner or the king.[64]

The statue owner's ability to participate via his '*statue-manifestations*' in the mentioned relationships with the living was surely an important religious motivation for having private statues made and set up in temples. The patrons must, however, also have realized the potential of the statues for negotiating identity within the elite group, thus using the '*statue-object*' as a means to show position, social relations, etc. In that way the royal donation of a statue to a subject for instance strengthened the relation between the king and the official receiving the statue. It positioned the receiver in relation to his peers, and probably created the wish among other officials to receive similar benefits, to mention a few examples of this.[65]

The statue thus served as a patient in relation to the patron, who had the statue made and decided the motif, material, etc., hence bringing about (through the statue) the immortalization

[64] Kjølby, *Temple Statues* I, pp. 62-76, 95-98; also Kjølby, 'Decision-Making and Structuration'.
[65] See Kjølby, *Temple Statues* I, pp. 95-98, 122-130, 149ff.

and provisioning of the person manifested. Through the image the patron thus had power over the statue owner (who could be himself or another), as it was for instance the patron who decided how the depicted should be remembered and represented (by the choice of motif, inscriptions, etc.), while it was the existence of the image that brought this about. The patron thus had the power to shape the distributed person of the statue owner.

Finally, we may include some of the relationships involving the artists or craftsmen, who acted as agents or patients in relation to the other participants. The production of a statue was made not by a single 'artist', but by teams of craftsmen or artists working under the supervision of one or more 'masters'.[66] In the following I shall however refer to this group of individuals by the common term 'artist':

Patron (A) -> artist (P)
Prototype (A) -> artist (P)
Statue (A) -> artist (P)

First of all, the patron, who could be identical with the owner or a donor, commissioned the statue, thereby causing the action of the artist. Secondly, the character and desired abilities of the owner and the appearance of various other 'prototypes', such as the mental image of an elite Egyptian or a vizier, were, as prototypes for the statue, influencing the decisions and actions of the artist.[67] Finally, the quality of the statue acted back on the artist by influencing his esteem, and possibly his payment or reward.[68]

However, the artist obviously also acted as an agent in relation to the other participants:

Artist (A) -> statue (P)
Artist (A) -> recipient (P)
Artist (A) -> prototype (P)

It was the artist who knew how to work according to the conventions, and how to work a specific material and model and finish the statue. The artist's technical and artistic skills therefore affected the quality and reception of the statue, and by creating the visual image the artist contributed to the maintenance of various mental images and to the remembrance and opinion of the statue owner amongst the living.[69]

The outlined agent/patient relationships do not cover all aspects of ancient Egyptian interactions between private statues and people, but illustrate the many relations involving statues and statue creation. However, the examples of 'material agency' implied by the discussion of statues in terms of agent/patient relationships are of different kinds.

Of the outlined relations the only ones that qualify as genuinely *experienced material agency* are the interactions between the statue-manifestation and the priests and passers-by, in which offerings and recitations are made to or for the person manifested, and in which the person, in his statue-manifestation, serves as mediator between the living and the gods. From an external analytic point of view these interactions between men and statue would be categorized as attributed material agency. While it is easy to accept that statues by their very presence

---

[66] Kjølby, 'Decision-Making and Structuration'.

[67] For the cooperation of craftsmen /artists during statue creation see Kjølby, *Temple Statues* I, pp. 196ff; Kjølby, 'Decision-Making and Structuration'.

[68] The latter is documented by a Deir el-Medina controversy concerning the payment of a statue see McDowell, A.G., *Village Life in Ancient Egypt. Laundry Lists and Love Songs*, Oxford 1999, pp. 82-83; Kjølby, *Temple Statues* I, p. 75.

[69] For immediate and long-term effects of statue creation see Kjølby, *Temple Statues* I, pp. 211ff.

exercise an influence on us as part of our life-world or material surroundings, statues and the dead cannot intentionally interact in the life of the living. In an Ancient Egyptian context there was, however, no clear distinction between a person and his statues. Private statues were, as already considered, material manifestations of a person, extending his presence in the world of the living. From an Egyptian point of view the agency exercised by private statues, or by the persons materialized or present in them, was thus not attributed by human beings, but experienced as real agency exercised by the person present in the statue.

The relation between the statue and the person manifested should not be defined as experienced material agency. Here the statue rather serves as an extension of the person materialized, distributing his person in time and space and thereby ensuring his immortality and ability to interact with the living.

Finally, looking at the patron–statue interactions, we see that these are examples of strategic human use of objects to achieve certain ends. This applies to the construction of a statue to serve as an eternal manifestation of the person represented, the making of the statue in a specific way, thus constructing the memory and appearance of the person, as well as for the use of the statues in the negotiation of identity amongst the living. The statues and their interaction with the statue owner and recipients must in this sense be seen as the extended or distributed agency of the patron, who may in several cases be identical with the person represented.

An understanding of material interaction also involves the more or less unrecognized influences on the living and their society by the statues as part of the world of the Egyptians, such as the reproduction of collective memory and consciousness of the past, the sense of group affiliation and identity, the maintenance of the mental images of an elite Egyptian, male, female etc. The choices made during statue creation thus resulted in various immediate and long-term effects, some of which would have been intended while others were the unexpected consequences of decisions made. The creation and use of private statues were thus involved in the reproduction of various religious, social, economic and representational practices and hence in the structuration of Egyptian society and the world of the statue-makers and their fellow Egyptians.[70] The interactions exemplified above are mostly immediate material interactions intended by the patrons, which means that the knowledge of the statues' ability to participate in these agent/patient relationships was part of the motivation for having a statue made and set up in a temple.

Conclusion

A New Kingdom private temple statue formed part of the distributed person of the individual represented or manifested in the statue. It served as a physical manifestation and contributed to the memory of his person, and extended his presence amongst and ability to interact with the living, thus ensuring his eternal well-being. This paper has focused on various forms of object-human interactions involving New Kingdom private temple statues. An identification of agent/patient relationships between the statue, artist, prototype (mental image or 'statue owner') and recipients (patron, priests and passers-by) emphasizes, how the statues played an active part in the world of the Egyptians as agents or patients in various interactions. Furthermore, a discussion of the character of the statues and perception of various statue-human interactions in terms of attributed and experienced agency, material influence and the object world as part of (and constituting) the extended or distributed person, mind and agency of human beings illustrates different aspects of 'material agency' and hence this aspect of ancient Egyptian materiality.

---

[70] Kjølby, *Temple Statues* I, pp. 211ff.

Self-perception and Self-assertion in the Portrait of Senwosret III

New methods for reading a face

Maya Müller

Introduction

The theme of this paper is the portrait of Senwosret III and its interpretation. This problem is, however, too complex to be discussed comprehensively in these few pages. Consequently I choose to present here a preliminary sketch of the methodological implications only. A full discussion of Senwosret III's portrait will be found in a study dealing with the royal sculpture of the Middle Kingdom, still in preparation, which will contain a chapter on the realistic royal faces from Senwosret II to Amenemhet III.

The entire study on Middle Kingdom sculpture on which I have been working for several years now comprises, on the one hand, discussions on the role of the people commissioning the statues, the sculptors, and the beholders as well as on the message of royal portraits as described in written sources. On the other hand, the statues themselves must be analysed in order to decipher the message and impact of their material and mimical properties, 'mimical properties' meaning the expression of the face and the signal language of the body.[1]

Senwosret III (ca. 1872-1853/52 BCE) is, however, an outstanding case. A new concept of the royal portrait appeared under this ruler: a fully realistic representation of the face. It carries a different message for the beholder than the statues of earlier kings with their synthetic physiognomies. The new portrait was created by an artist who perceived the king in a different way. This act presupposes that the king perceived himself in a different way. An imposing portrait is the product of the self-perception of the model and the perception of an important artist.

The four points of the paper are the following:

1. What is new in the portrait of Senwosret III, and how did previous research deal with it?

2. How can a face be analysed with (a sufficient) objectivity, without knowing anything about the personality represented or disregarding the foreknowledge about him? We distinguish six sub points:

2.1. The genetically determined face.
2.2. Biologically determined beauty.
2.3. Biologically conditioned aging.
2.4. Biologically conditioned expressions of primary emotions.

[1] Part of this programme has been carried out and published in the first issue of *Imago Aegypti*. In this article, one finds, among several of the above mentioned points, a discussion of the mimical properties of Mentuhotep II, III and Senwosret I (Müller, Maya, "Die Königsplastik des Mittleren Reiches und ihre Schöpfer: Reden über Statuen - Wenn Statuen reden", *Imago Aegypti* 1 (2005), PP. 27-78.

2.5. Biologically conditioned sign language of the body.
2.6. Interim results

3. Personal expression. What can we read from a face when having sufficient knowledge about the character of the personality represented? This includes three sub points:

3.1. What are the results of previous attempts to interpret the face of Senwosret III?
3.2. We make a check-test: Examining the pictures of famous modern men who resemble Senwosret III can help us in defining the relation between character and facial expression in well-documented cases, these personalities serving as substitutes for Senwosret of whom we know little.
3.3. We analyse the royal texts of Senwosret III, presuming that they can provide some information on his character.

4. Finally, the conclusion provides some preliminary remarks on royal self-perception, as perceived and 'translated' into stone by artists.

1. The new concept of the royal portrait

Our first point concerns the new concept of the royal portrait as it can be observed on some relatively well preserved heads such as the obsidian head in Lisbon, the small Berlin head 20175, and the Gallatin head in New York.[2] The face seems to be worked out in a realistic manner, as if the sculptor had taken a plaster cast of the living king and gone over it again. I have the sensation of looking at a photo, whereas all previous kings were represented with a synthetically composed face, partially mask-like, and partially organic.

The lifelike modelling of a face was not a new invention of the 12th Dynasty. There are precursors in the private sculpture of the Old Kingdom, chiefly the famous bust of Ankhhaf in Boston.[3] The appearance of a realistic royal face has, however, provoked many comments ever since it was discovered by Egyptologists about one hundred years ago. Scholars attempted to read the expression of the face which was seen as reflecting the nature and character of the king, assuming that it was a true rendering of reality.[4] Previous researchers treated the matter intuitively, sometimes neglecting analyses and argumentation, but delivering statements about the expressions of the king's face.[5] Such assertions may be plausible; they are, however, arbitrary. This is where I want to set in; presuming that there must exist, for any definable problem, a way of analysing it.

The readers of this article should, however, keep in mind that there is a fundamental difference between analysing a statue, even if realistically rendered, and a living person, and that a statue is not a passport photo, but rather a work of art.

---

[2] Lisbon, Museu Calouste Gulbenkian 138 (Lange, K., Sesostris. *Ein ägyptischer König in Mythos, Geschichte und Kunst*, München 1954, p. 48, pl. 26-27); Berlin, Ägyptisches Museum, Inv. 20175 (lost in Second World War) (Lange, K., *Sesostris*, pl. 22-23); New York, Metropolitan Museum of Art 66.99.5 (Aldred, C., "Some Royal Portraits of the Middle Kingdom", in: *Metropolitan Museum Journal* 3 (1970), p. 43, fig. 23-24).

[3] Boston, Museum of Fine Arts 27442 (Schulz, R. / Seidel, M., *Ägypten. Die Welt der Pharaonen*, Köln 1997, p. 103, fig. 106 (4th dyn., ca. 2500 BCE).

[4] Keeping in mind that we have no formal proof that the owner of this face was indeed king Senwosret III.

[5] See below, 3.1.

2. Analysing face and body

How can the face and the body of a statue be analysed? First of all, the 'topography' of a head must be described in detail, comprising all the lines, forms and proportions which constitute the features. We can distinguish, as far as I can see today, five levels or aspects which are valid for all cases of realistic rendering (not only for the second half of the 12th Dynasty):

(1) The features as they are inherited from the parents: in other words, the genetically determined face.
(2) The biologically conditioned expression of beauty in the sense of sexual attractivity.
(3) The signs of biologically conditioned ageing.
(4) The biologically conditioned expressions of primary emotions, (such as happiness, sadness, anger etc.), which seemingly are the same all over the world.
(5) The sign language of the body, consisting, in the case of Senwosret III, chiefly of the biologically conditioned expression of beauty.
(6) Interim results after analysis of biologically conditioned factors.

2.1. The genetically determined face

For the analysis of the face of Senwosret III, we can only use more or less complete heads where the nose is well preserved. Fragmentary heads[6] deceive too much since lines are blurred, proportions altered etc. We first describe the 'general topography' of the face, corresponding to what I called the genetically determined face, supposing that the sculptors intended a recognizable image. The best examples are two of the relatively young looking heads, Berlin 20175 (fig. 3) and Lisbon MCG 138[7] (fig. 7), which possibly render the look of the king as conceived at the beginning of his reign. The following description refers to a fully frontal view, 'right' and 'left' from the point of view of the beholder.

It is a large, rectangular face, the contour of which is defined by the high cheek-bones and the angles of the lower jaw. There is no spot on the surface without modelling. The eyes are highly placed in relation to the total height of the head. The upper lid area is hollowed out, the upper contour being a furrow, the curve of which reaches its accent, i.e. the point of strongest curvature, near the outer end. The eyebrow runs tightly above the upper eyelid, being nearly straight and horizontal; after reaching its accent near the outward end, it slopes steeply downward. The eyeball is protruding so that the upper and lower eyelids are convex. The axis of the eye (running straight from the inner corner to the outer) slopes slightly downward toward the outside. The borders of the upper and lower eyelids are relatively straight. If we follow the borderline of the upper lid from the inner to the outer end, we find the point of strongest curvature closely before the line has made half its way, and when observing the border of the lower lid, we find the accent closely after having made half the way. To sum up, there is a sophisticated play of shifted accents and of slightly bent and chiefly sloping lines, conferring a very unusual configuration to Senwosret's eye area.

The bridge of the nose is narrow, the wings triangular (not bulging), the tip small (the nose of the Berlin head is very slightly damaged). There are folds from the corners of the eyes into the cheeks, and nasal labial folds. The highly placed cheek-bones form a ridge toward the temples. The clearly drawn borders of the relatively thin lips approach the shape of a lozenge, the slit is horizontal, one corner pointing slightly downward. The contours of the mouth are, however, delicately curvilinear and the lips padded by a subcutaneous fatty layer. The circular

[6] E.g. Paris, Louvre E 25370 (Delange, E., *Musée du Louvre. Catalogue des statues égyptiennes du Moyen Empire*, Paris 1987, pp. 44-45, 3 figs.); New York, Metropolitan Museum of Art 26.7.1394, the famous Carnarvon head (Lange, K., *Sesostris*, p. 49, pl.36).
[7] See note 2.

muscle around the corners is also finely padded. The lower lip ends at its lower side in a bent furrow which marks the border between lip and chin bulge, (this furrow becoming angular, with aging). The tight chin-bulge is oval-rectangular. The face is characterized, moreover, by slight asymmetries, the corners of the eye and the mouth sloping more to the right.

Profile view: The forehead is slightly convex. There is a small recess at the root of the nose, the projection of the nose is medium-sized, the base line of the nose slightly rising toward the tip. The upper lip is relatively long (beginning at the septum), the lower short; the lower lip recedes strongly, as does the chin-bulge beginning in the above-mentioned furrow. The base of the chin is descending toward the neck.

2.2. Biologically determined beauty

We now come to the biologically conditioned expressions, beginning with beauty in the sense of sexual attractivity. This matter ought to be explained at length because of its impact on our understanding of Egyptian portraiture. This cannot be done here for reasons of space. Instead, I must refer the reader to the literature,[8] giving here the shortest possible description of the relevant points. We are dealing with results of recent research demonstrating that the perception of physical beauty is indeed biologically conditioned. According to Etkoff[9] and Richter,[10] an aesthetic selection of body and face went on during the evolution of mankind, developing an ideal of beauty. The sexually most attractive partner is the one with the best physical and mental capacities for mastering life, with health and intelligence being the most wanted properties. These are recognizable on the face at a specific normalized configuration occurring in a masculine and a feminine variant.

Applying the rules of the masculine configuration to the face of Senwosret III, the following of his physical properties belong to masculine beauty: the quasi-rectangular contour of the face, the highly placed eyes which stand well apart and have a horizontal axis, the scarcely bent eyebrows, the straight slit of the mouth, the slightly curvilinear and slightly padded lips, and the narrow nose. Thus, there are signs of beauty in Senwosret's face. The features of most of his statues reflect, however, a phase of life far beyond the age in which sexual attractivity is most important. It is a phase of maturity, when the mental background of beauty takes effect, the expression of beauty turning into intelligence and distinction.

2.3. Biologically conditioned aging

As to the signs of aging in a face, there is of course no need to explain that they are biologically conditioned. When looking for example at two famous heads from Medamud,[11] Louvre E 12962 and Cairo CG 486, there are obvious signs of aging: Folds are deeper, there is a triangular hollow below the eye, the outer ends of eye, brow and mouth are more strongly slanted downward. The nose, lips and chin-bulge become longer since the slacking tissue sinks

---

[8] Eibl-Eibesfeldt, I., "The Biological Foundation of Aesthetics", in: Rentschler, I. / Herzberger, B. / Epstein, D. (eds.), *Beauty and the Brain. Biological Aspects of Aesthetics*, Basel / Boston / Berlin 1988, pp. 40-43; Etkoff, Nancy, Survival of the Prettiest – The Science of Beauty, New York 1999; Richter, Klaus, *Die Herkunft des Schönen. Grundzüge der evolutionären Ästhetik*, Mainz 1999, particularly pp. 45-51, 74, 116-121; Müller, Maya, "Schönheitsideale in der ägyptischen Kunst", in: Györy, H. (ed.), *"Le lotus qui sort de terre". Mélanges offerts à Edith Varga*, Bulletin du Musée Hongrois des Beaux-Arts, Supplément-2001, Budapest 2001, pp. 239-286.

[9] See note 8.

[10] See note 8. Neither Etkoff nor Richter provides a paradigmatic view of a modern masculin face corresponding to the biologically conditioned ideal of beauty. It is extremely difficult to find, in pertinent periodicals or books, useful photos of beautiful men for we need a plain frontal view of a face without facial hair, and a relaxed mouth without a smile. See e.g. the actor Laurence Olivier in: Warren, P., *British Film Studios. An Illustrated History*, 2nd ed. London 2001, fig. on p. 36.

[11] Paris, Louvre E 12962 (Lange, K., *Sesostris*, p. 50, pl. 38; Delanges, E., *Catalogue des statues égyptiennes du Moyen Empire*, p. 29, 1 fig.), Cairo, Egyptian Museum CG 486 (Lange, K., *Sesostris*, p. 49, pl. 37).

down. This last symptom is, however, virtually not perceptible on Senwosret's heads, a fact which probably means that he was not more than middle aged.[12] On other statues, e.g. the series from the temple of Mentuhotep II at Deir el-Bahari,[13] the folds and asymmetries are more marked, the ears are bigger and strongly sticking out. These features are, however, not the symptoms of high age, but can be interpreted, to my mind, as stylistic means of an outstanding artist expressing his personal view of the king's character, every statue being not only a true rendering of the portrait as laid down in the beginning of the reign, but also an individual interpretation of a specific artist.

2.4. The biologically conditioned expression of primary emotions

The expression of basic emotions is, like that of beauty in the sense of sexual attractivity, biologically conditioned and universal. Again, I cannot go into details but must refer the reader to the literature. Recent research on facial expression distinguishes seven primary emotions which are expressed mimically in the same way all over the globe:[14] Happiness, sadness, fear, anger, surprise, contempt, and disgust. In contrast to this, feelings like depression, disillusion or sorrow, which are often assigned to Senwosret III in Egyptological literature, are complex emotions which cannot be rendered by plain contractions and dilations of the facial muscles. That is why there can be no proof of their presence in the face of a statue. As long as we have no proof from literary sources, it is pure speculation.[15] Two statues of the series found in the temple of Mentuhotep II at Deir el-Bahari (British Museum EA 685 and 686)[16] show two quite different interpretations of the king's nature. No. 686 is the most impressive case of eyebrows, eye axes and corners of the mouth slanting steeply down. Moreover, the asymmetries are accentuated, the left eye being higher, the lines of the right side slanting steeper. The slanting lines are of course the conventional and universal expression of sadness, the statue EA 685 exhibiting a slight sadness, EA 686 a deeper one. I think the important fact is that the faces of the king show emotions at all because this is sign of his sensibility. We even have a further indication: The whole surface of the big ears and the face is strongly modelled, the muscular structure being visible everywhere. This undulating movement suggests that the king was capable of quick and differentiated reaction to stimuli, when communicating with people.

2.5. Sign language of the body

The signs of body language in Senwosret III's statues must unfortunately be interpreted on a very limited basis, since very few examples of the king's body are preserved, either in sculpture or in relief, and none are complete. I can cite only a colossal statue from Karnak (Cairo CG 42011) which is nearly complete, and a relief fragment from the Hebsed gate at Medamud (Cairo JE 56497) which allow some conclusions.[17] The king's body is much more realistic than those of previous kings. However, the sign language is very restricted because the statue Cairo

---

[12] I estimate the age of the younger faces to about 40, and of the elder ones to about 50 years. These are avarage values, in individual cases it can be several years more or less. For the elder heads of Senwosret III, compare e.g. the face of Maximilian Schell at the age of c. 53 in the Film "Peter the Great", with marked folds though without slacking tissue, having a certain resemblance with Senwosret III.

[13] London British Museum EA 685-687, and Cairo RT 18/4/22/4.

[14] Ekman, Paul, "Facial Signs: Facts, Fantasies and Possibilities", in: Sebeok, Th. (ed.), *Sight, Sound, and Sense*, Indiana 1978, pp. 124-156; Ekman, P. (ed.), *Emotion in the Human Face* (second edition), Cambridge 1982.

[15] A European work of art, Renaissance or later, can eventually express depressivity through movements or gestures which the Egyptian system of representation does not allow, such as sagging shoulders or a hanging head (see 2.5.).

[16] London, British Museum EA 684, 685, 686 (Polz, F., "Die Bildnisse Sesostris' III. und Amenemhets III.", in: *Mitteilungen des Deutschen Archäologischen Instituts Kairo* 51 (1995), pp. 227-254, pl. 48a-b (EA 686, 684).

[17] Cairo CG 42011 (Evers, H., *Staat aus dem Stein. Denkmäler, Geschichte und Bedeutung der ägyptischen Plastik während des Mittleren Reichs*, München 1929, pl. 80); Cairo JE 56497 (Vandersleyen, C. (ed.), *Das alte Ägypten*, Propyläen Kunstgeschichte vol. 15, Berlin 1975, pl. 277).

CG 42011 complies with the Egyptian rules of representation which strictly respect the mirror symmetrical structure of the body, never allowing any tortional movement or gesture. The shoulders, the chest and the neck are broad, the hips narrow, the legs stout. The muscular structure is worked out in deep relief. The whole figure is strong and athletic, if somewhat stout. This physique comes relatively near to the biologically conditioned ideal of masculine beauty in the sense of sexual attractivity. Some Egyptologists have suggested that the body is idealized and looks much younger than the face. I am, however, not convinced that this is true for the statue Cairo CG 42011. In any case, the body conveys the impression of strength, energy, and self-assertion.

2.6. Interim results

What can we say about the expression of the king's portrait after analysing the biologically conditioned factors? We saw that the face betrays emotion, thus captivating the interest of the beholder who wishes to understand and to respond. The body build and bearing betray strength and power. As to the facial features, we found important signs of beauty which signal, in the mature configuration of a middle-aged or elderly man, intelligence and distinction. To sum up, we can speak of a distinguished, intelligent, energetic and sensitive personality.

3. Personal expression

The personal expression is formed, in reality, with increasing age by the experience of life and by the character of the person represented which modify or stamp the features in an individual manner. It can be studied by comparing the character of a historical personality as known from written sources with the facial features. This is no easy task in the case of Senwosret III since we know little about him, having few royal texts from his reign. Moreover, it is difficult to decide how far these texts are purely conventional or how far they are inspired by the king himself, containing a personal message.

3.1. Previous attempts to interpret the face of Senwosret III

Let us have a quick look at the interpretations of previous scholars. For the last 80 years, archaeologists and Egyptologists repeatedly came back, when describing Senwosret III's statues, to the same set of keywords. They are of two kinds, a 'pessimistic' and an 'optimistic' one, some scholars using both at one time.[18]

The chief 'pessimistic' keywords are: sorrow, depression, tiredness, disillusion, senility, pessimism, bitterness, grief, and resignation. An early representative of the 'pessimistic' interpretation is Ludwig Curtius (1923) who speaks of melancholy, tiredness, deep pessimism, and tragical shock, while Assmann perceives, in 1990, the expression of resignation, bitterness, and melancholy in Senwosret's face.

As to the 'optimistic' series, we chiefly find: striving for power, triumphant strength, self-consciousness, energy, responsibility, self-command, humaneness, will-power, and determination. Hans Georg Evers, in 1928, calls Senwosret's statues the incorporation of the state cut in stone, representing triumphant power and a hero free of illusion. Wildung believes

[18] Here a few examples: Curtius, Ludwig, *Die antike Kunst: Ägypten und Vorderasien*, Handbuch der Kunstwissenschaft, Berlin Neubabelsberg 1923 (written 1913); Evers, H., *Staat aus dem Stein*, chiefly pp. 18, 66, 85-88, 104-109; Otto, Eberhard, *Ägypten. Der Weg des Pharaonenreichs*, 4th ed. Stuttgart 1966, p. 124; Wolf, W., *Die Kunst Ägyptens. Gestalt und Geschichte*, Stuttgart 1957, pp. 236, 327-328, 394: Wildung, D., *Sesostris und Amenemhet. Ägypten im Mittleren Reich*, 1984, p. 203; Assmann, J., "Ikonologie der Identität", in: Kraatz, M. / Seckel, D. (eds), *Das Bildnis in der Kunst des Orients*, Stuttgart 1990, 17-43; Delia, R. D., "Khakaure Senwosret III: King and Man", *KMT* 6/2 (1995), pp. 26-27, 31.

that the perported tragedy and melancholy of this ruler turns into resolute power policy and undisturbed self-consciousness, when considering the royal texts (1988).

Scholars gave, in many cases, no arguments for their statements. This is particularly true for the 'pessimistic' series, whereas the supporters of the 'optimistic' series could find corroborating evidence in royal texts from the reign of Senwosret III.

3.2. Check-test with portraits of modern personalities resembling Senwosret III, serving as 'substitutes' for the king

The following is a kind of cross-check. I sought a way to find out how far the face of an 'elder statesman' or scholar reflects his personality and character. For obvious reasons, a test can only be made with modern individuals of whom we have portraits of sufficient quality as well as extensive evidence of their life and character. Such individuals can only be relevant for the case of Senwosret III if there is a close physical resemblance of their faces with his. That is why I suggest studying the portraits of four modern men who meet three conditions: They must have a good resemblance with Senwosret III, they must be important personalities who were professionally active in public, and their course of life and character must be very well known.
This test has nothing to do with physiognomical theories which have existed since the late Roman republic and seem to be of different kinds, especially in the 18th and 19th centuries. Physiognomists normally define a number of specific physical properties which invariably betray specific mental properties. It is important to note, for our context, that they claim to read the character of persons totally unknown to them, observing their body and bearing. In direct opposition to this, my test concerns prominent men whose character is described to us by authorities on the basis of original documents or personal acquaintance. I then try to find out whether some important mental characteristics of each of these personalities can be recognised in their facial features. This is a new experiment whose usefulness should be tested. Again, I can only give here a rudimentary sketch of the results I obtained.

Our first candidate is the Swiss general Guillaume-Henri Dufour (1787-1875), an officer, politician, engineer and cartographer.[19] He became famous for his role in the last Swiss civil war of 1847: As general of the federate troops, he succeeded in bringing the war to an early end through his intelligent tactics and negotiation. Subsequently, his wise diplomacy led to the foundation of Switzerland, in 1848, and he was one of the founders of the Red Cross in 1864. He is described, in the sources cited in Langendorf's biography, as a man of keen analytical intelligence, far-sighted, courageous, one who can deal with power, using his aggressive potential (and force in general) in a controlled way to avoid more bloodshed. He is said to have been incorruptible, a man of action, sensibility, humaneness, and a passionate scientist, having a strict sense of duty, and a firm self-assertion.

Dufour's portrait bust by James Pradier (1849) (fig. 2)[20] can be compared to the king's sitting statue from Medamud Cairo JE 32639 (fig. 1).[21] Dufour is older on his portraits than Senwosret, he is around 60, a fact which makes comparison more difficult. The lower half of Dufour's face is slightly narrower, the folds deeper, otherwise the features compare quite well. The profiles of the two personalities are astonishingly similar, judging from the medal by Bory[22] of ca 1850 and

---

[19] Many portraits are published in printed biographies and on the internet; a "biography in pictures" is: Langendorf, J.-J., *Guillaume-Henri Dufour, General - Kartograph - Humanist. Eine Bildbiographie*, Zürich 1987, citing many primary sources such as letters by and to Dufour.

[20] Langendorf, J.-J., *Guillaume-Henri Dufour*, fig. on p.143, see also the drawing of the head by his daughter Annette, fig. on p. 135.

[21] Lange, K., *Sesostris*, 49, pl. 34-35.

[22] Langendorf, J.-J., *Guillaume-Henri Dufour*, fig. on p. 71r.

Fig. 1: Senusret III, Cairo Egyptian Museum JE 32639, from Medamud, granite (from: Lange, K., *Sesostris. Ein ägyptischer König in Mythos, Geschichte und Kunst*, Hirmer Verlag, München 1954, pl. 34)

Fig. 2: Guillaume-Henri Dufour, bust by James Pradier, 1849 (from: Langendorf, J.-J., *Guillaume-Henri Dufour. General - Kartograph - Humanist*, Schweizer Verlagshaus, Zürich 1987, fig. on p. 143).

Fig. 3: Senusret III, Berlin Ägyptisches Museum 20175 (lost), provenance unknown, schist (from: Lange, K., *Sesostris. Ein ägyptischer König in Mythos, Geschichte und Kunst*, Hirmer Verlag, München 1954, pl. 23).

Fig. 4: George C. Marshall, photo, 1938 (from: Cray, Ed, General of the Army, *George C. Marshall Soldier and Statesman*, W. W. Norton & Company, New York / London 1990, fig. on p. 289 upper).

the well-preserved Berlin head 20175.[23] The only difference which concerns the mouth is due to the far higher age of Dufour whose lips have lost their protruding subcutaneous fat pads.

Our second example, General George Marshall (1880-1959),[24] was a professional soldier, a military academy teacher, an important strategist and organizer in the First and Second World Wars, the inventor of the Marshall-plan, foreign secretary, and was awarded the Nobel Peace Prize in 1953. US President Truman said: 'He is the greatest American of our days'. His chief qualities are a brilliant intellect, absolute integrity, steadfastness and self-control, and the use of force only to achieve ethically justified goals, according to the sources cited in his biographies.

Comparing a photo (fig. 4)[25] of 1938 taken when he was 58 to the Berlin head 20175 (fig. 3),[26] we mainly note the similar configuration of the eyes with the axis slightly slanting downward, and the fine mouth with horizontal corners. There is a little difference in that Marshall's eye sockets are somewhat less deep and the jaws are more tapering toward the chin.

The third example is Tadeusz Mazowiecki (born 1927)[27] whose photo (fig. 6)[28] of about 1993 can best be compared to one of the king's granite statues from Deir el-Bahari (British Museum EA 686) (fig. 5).[29] A Polish lawyer, journalist and politician, he was Member of Parliament from 1961 on and active in several organisations as a critic of the regime; adviser of Solidarnosc, he became prime minister of free Poland in 1989. Later he stood up for human rights, writing a book on 'moral in politics'; always struggling for the rule of law and justice, courageous, incorruptible, endowed with a strong will-power, if we choose to believe the words of his admirers. Although Mazowiecki looks older (he is over sixty), the resemblance with Senwosret III is striking, including the asymmetry of the eye-region, one eye being higher placed than the other. The king's Deir el-Bahari statue represents an unusually personal style, showing a set of particular properties: The general relief or modelling of the face including the big ears is more accentuated, the downward tendency of the sloping lines is enhanced, as is the angularity of forms in the eye region (see descriptions in 2.1. and 2.3.). Most striking is perhaps the expression of will-power, self-control and energy.

Our fourth example is Jacob Wackernagel (1853-1938),[30] professor of classical languages, Sanskrit and linguistics at Basel university, whom we know from a photo (fig. 8)[31] of ca. 1910 which can be set at the side of Senwosret III's obsidian head at Lisbon (fig. 7).[32] According to the obituary written by a colleague, he was an outstanding scholar and charismatic personality, very rich in knowledge and ideas and a generous communicator, free of envy; excelling in energy, integrity, sensibility, and goodness.

---

[23] Lange, K., *Sesostris*, p. 48, pl.22. The tip of the nose is very slightly chipped. The base of the nose is in fact slightly rising from the septum to the tip. See also the reliefs from Medamud (Vandersleyen, C. (ed.), *Ägypten*, pl. 277a-b).

[24] Cray, Ed, *General of the Army, George C. Marshall Soldier and Statesman*, New York / London 1990; Pujo, Bernard, *Le général George C. Marshall (1880-1959): Par deux fois il a sauvé l'Europe*, Paris 2003.

[25] Cray, Ed, *General of the Army*, fig. on p. 289 (upper).

[26] Lange, K., *Sesostris*, 48, pl. 23.

[27] Articles "Tadeusz Mazowiecki" in Polish, English and German, in the on-line encyclopedia *Wikipedia*; *Encyclopaedia Britannica Online*, Article 9051642 (retrieved March 1, 2008).

[28] Photo in the journal *Basler Zeitung* of 09.10.1993.

[29] Polz, F., *Die Bildnisse Sesostris' III. und Amenemhets III.*, pl. 48a.

[30] Sommer, F., "Jacob Wackernagel (11.12.1853 – 22.05.1938)", in: *Sitzungsberichte der phil.-hist. Abteilung der Bayerischen Akademie der Wissenschaften zu München*, Jahrgang 1939 (Heft 11), München 1939, pp. 23-26; Antidoron, *Festschrift Jacob Wackernagel*, Göttingen 1923.

[31] Bieri, S. / Heuser, M. (eds), *Vom General zum Glamour Girl. Ein Porträt der Schweiz*, Basel 2005, fig. 50.

[32] Lisbon, Museu Calouste Gulbenkian 138 (Lange, K., *Sesostris*, 48, pl. 27).

What I see in his face is distinction, keen intelligence, energy, and perhaps goodness (instead of the aggressive potential of the previously cited examples). The last may be induced through the slightly bent position of the head and the pensive gesture of the right hand. This gesture is of course not a facial expression but a signal of the body. Gestures based on tortional movements were, however, not admitted in the Egyptian canon of representation.

Comparing the four modern men, we find an interesting convergence of properties. They all have a keen analytical intelligence, an aura of distinction, and an energy including an aggressive potential; they are vigorous, incorruptible, just, sensitive, humane, and self-controlled, using power or force only to achieve ethically justified goals. The qualities either coincide with the four basic properties we found in Senwosret's face (intelligence, distinction, energy, and sensibility), or they are more complex derivatives of them. It seems to me that the complex inner qualities can indeed be localised in the face of a ripe personality.

To come back to Senwosret III, there is a general consensus among Egyptologists that the king's character can indeed be read from his traits, although their intuitive interpretation does not allow verification (see above 3.1.). Our aim is, however to define which forms and lines of the face are responsible for which expression. Generally, the most personal marks are found in the regions of the eyes and the mouth, for these are the most expressive areas, being the seats of vision and speech. Such personal marks are probably formed by an individual 'training' of the mimical muscles over many years, and they are at the same time the result of the biologically conditioned properties of the face as defined above in 2.1.-5.

Comparing our four modern personalities' and Senwosret's faces, I believe I can establish the following relations of specific physical traits with specific expressions. (For terminology, see the description of Senwosret's face in 2.1.): Some important elements of the face are nearly horizontal, especially the axes of the eyes, the inner parts of the eyebrows and the split of the mouth; furthermore, the contour of the face is tendentially rectangular. These lines, together with the spacey length of the face, give an impression of balance, harmony, and composure. In combination with the pronounced cheek-bones and corners of the lower jaws, they also have an effect of energy and vitality. The mouth with the moderately padded lips, the moderately curvilinear lip borders, and the clearly drawn contour, looks relaxed and disciplined, sensitive and self-possessed. The same is true for the nose with the narrow bridge, the small tip and the triangular wings, the mouth and the nose betraying, moreover, intelligence and self-control.

When the axis of the eyes slopes slightly outward downward, and when the outer ends of the eyebrows and the folds which are situated below the eyes, nose and mouth slope diagonally downward, the effect is a slight sadness which can be understood as a sign of humaneness and sensibility.

The last set of relevant properties is inherent in the configuration of the eye region, (as described in 2.1.), which is characterised by a sophisticated play of shifted accents and of relatively straight and sloping lines. Further characteristics are eyeballs protruding from relatively deep sockets, and eyebrows casting shadows over them, thus giving 'depth' to the look. These properties confer a forceful relief and angularity to the eye region, producing an effect which can be described as masculine, energetic, intelligent, distinguished, and potentially aggressive.

3.3. The royal texts of Senwosret III

This leads us to the written sources from the reign of Senwosret III, which are indeed very scant. There is the Semna-Stela, found in the temple of the Second Cataract fort at Semna, and

Fig. 5: Senusret III, London British Museum EA 686, from Deir el-Bahari, granite (courtesy, The British Museum).

Fig. 6: Tadeusz Mazowiecki, photo, ca. 1993 (from: *Basler Zeitung*, 09.10.1993)

Fig. 7: Senusret III, Lisbon Museu Calouste Gulbenkian 138, provenance unknown, obsidian (from: Lange, K., Sesostris. *Ein ägyptischer König in Mythos, Geschichte und Kunst*, Hirmer Verlag, München 1954, pl. 27).

Fig. 8: Jacob Wackernagel, linguist, photo by Albert Teichmann, ca. 1910 (from: Bieri, S. / Heuser, M. (eds), *Vom General zum Glamour Girl. Ein Porträt der Schweiz*, Schwabe Verlag, Basel 2005, fig. 50). © Graphische Sammlung, Schweizerische Nationalbibliothek Bern

a cycle of hymns in praise of the king, from one of the Lahun papyri. Both texts seem to be inspired by the king himself.[33]

The Semna-stela is a very personal text insofar as it is a political manifesto, explaining the king's doctrine on his power politics in Nubia, and as such a unique document.[34] There is not the slightest religious aspect. It is pure *Realpolitik* and a rational explanation of his tactics. Senwosret considers the definite establishment of his southern border at Semna as his lifework which he proudly propagates. The stela briefly explains that the Nubians, (as well as all other enemies), are cowards, craven-hearted, aggressive wretches who deserve not to live but must be smitten without mercy. Senwosret's work, the empire in Nubia, must last forever. His sons must maintain and defend it, otherwise he threatens to repudiate them for they are unworthy. The text now tells us that the king had a statue made of himself and installed on the border, in the sanctuary of Semna, in order to grant that his will is respected forever. Senwosret III acts with the outmost decision, creating a great work: "I am a king whose word (or plan) becomes act", he says. Force and extermination against enemies is justified, to the ancient Egyptian mind, by the infamy of the Nubians who dared attacking the legitimate ruler of the world. Interestingly, the stela explicitly states that the king is considerate with clients and steady in mercy.

The four hymns in praise of the king give a poetic picture of his political merits.[35] His aim is made very clear: He protects the land and extends its boundaries. The description of his gigantic physical strength and size is most impressive: He grasps the two lands with his hands, and he has a million of hands. His terrible radiation slays all his foes without using a weapon, though he also uses the bow like Sekhmet. It is his plan or command which effects what he wants. He cares for all inhabitants as does a father, since he is their begetter and provider, making them rich and happy. He is a protector like a mountain or a fortress (etc.). Every deed of his is a triumphant success.

The picture of the king as provided by the hymns is a personal one insofar as a significant number of metaphors refer to his physical appearance. We need not deal here with the abstract levels of meaning of these metaphors since it is just the material nature of the comparisons describing his body, his aura, his gigantic stature, or his 'architectural' or 'landscape-like' build, which is relevant for our context. This is a feature not found in previous royal hymns. Admitting that pertinent texts from earlier reigns are rare, I think there is a chance that some of the metaphors and the combination of themes in the cycle of hymns were created for Senwosret III.

Both texts give us to understand that the king is well conscious of his power, in the physical and in the mental sense. His way of exercising might is sovereign and mostly controlled by reason, whether attacking his enemies or caring for the well-being of his subjects. In both texts, there are references to the king's feelings: On the Semna-stela, we meet with Senwosret's contempt for his enemies and his emotional relation to his sons whom he suspects to be untrue; in the hymns, we find a fatherly attitude toward his subjects who depend on his care and sustenance.

---

[33] Compare Delia, R. D., "Khakaure Senwosret III: King and Man", *KMT* 6/2 (1995), pp. 19-33.

[34] Parkinson, Richard, *Voices from Ancient Egypt. An Anthology of Middle Kingdom Writings*, London 1991, pp. 43-46; Lichtheim, M., *Ancient Egyptian Literature I: The Old and Middle Kingdoms*, Berkeley 1973, pp. 118-120; a virtually identical stela was found at Uronarti (Janssen, J.M.A., "The stela (Khartoum Museum no. 3) from Uronarti", *JNES* 12 (1953), pp. 51-55).

[35] Quirke, St., *Egyptian Literature 1800 BC, Questions and Readings*, London 2004, pp. 203-205; Assmann, J., *Ägyptische Hymnen und Gebete*, Zürich / München 1975, pp. 476-480.

4. Conclusion

What can we say about the expression of Senwosret's face now, after having examined the statues, some comparable modern 'substitute' portraits, and the royal texts?

The four properties as defined in our point 2 can now be differentiated, (if only with due caution):

- Distinction is joined by self-command, incorruptibility (there are no signs of greed in any sense), and controlled use of force for morally (or at least politically) justified goals.
- Intelligence goes with authority.
- Energy and activity are intense enough to suggest an aggressive potential.
- Sensibility goes with humaneness.

What can we say about the manner in which the king perceived himself?

The statues of Senwosret III bear evidence of his self-perception, for they have an individual face betraying specific properties of his character. Senwosret III is able to perceive his own self and to show it (or to have it shown by his artists and writers) because he was interested in it and assigned it a high value. There is, of course, no royal text containing such an assertion; it is, however, a logical deduction from the sources. Nevertheless, the text of the Semna-stela provides a hint which is hidden in the story of Senwosret's statue installed on the boundary, for the story betrays his feelings. We learn that the king regarded his deed, namely the definite establishment of the southern border at Semna, as a personal concept wholly arisen from his own genius. Likewise, the king's relation with his sons is described as an emotional one, thus bringing about the singular idea of a statue with a political function, serving as a memorial. A beholder who looked at such a statue could know the king by his face, without needing an inscription of the name. It is a well-known fact that a portrait with a personal and emotional expression appeals to the emotions of the beholder, captivating his interest and provoking a personal response. The message of Senwosret's statue is his individual aura (as described above), becoming the paradigm for the behaviour of beholders, such as those looking at the boundary statue of Semna.

Taking Phenomenology to Heart

Some heuristic remarks on studying ancient Egyptian embodied experience*

Rune Nyord

A very important trend in the humanities and social sciences of the late 20th and early 21st centuries is that of theory-building with a basis in the philosophical tradition of phenomenology. In their various guises, such approaches have given researchers a renewed interest in phenomena such as bodies, perception and embodied experience, and have had a particularly noticeable influence in anthropology and archaeology under the heading of "materiality", which attempts to transcend a number of familiar philosophical dichotomies.[1] In contrast to the study of material culture, where the turn towards the materiality of objects can be more readily implemented, it seems on the surface much more difficult to incorporate the insights of phenomenology into philological research, as there is a substantial methodological gap to be bridged between phenomenological experiences on the one hand and abstract linguistic expressions on the other. On closer scrutiny of the theoretical literature, however, it becomes apparent that this gap is far from as insurmountable as it might seem initially. First, advances in cognitive linguistics and experimental psychology have shown that even our most abstract thinking is deeply rooted in experiences of the human body, from whence abstract concepts acquire both structure and axiology.[2] Secondly, language gives access to the conceptualization of inchoate experiences, and as such constitutes a crucial medium for phenomenological *being-in-the-world*, in the words of the phenomenological philosopher Maurice Merleau-Ponty (1908-1961):

> Il [sc. language] présente ou plutôt il est la prise de position du sujet dans le monde de ses significations. Le terme 'monde' n'est pas ici une manière de parler : il veut dire que la vie 'mentale' ou culturelle emprunte à la vie naturelle ses structures et que le sujet pensant doit être fondé sur le sujet incarné.[3]

In light of this promising point of departure, the question becomes how to develop a methodology which makes it possible to go from the level of philological analysis to that of studying phenomenological aspects of embodied experience. What is needed here is primarily a vocabulary of embodiment and a conceptual apparatus which makes it possible to correlate linguistic expressions with particular experiential elements. In this paper, it will be proposed that the "New Phenomenology" of the German philosopher Hermann Schmitz (born 1928), which includes what he calls an "Alphabet der Leiblichkeit", offers just such an opportunity.

---

* I am grateful to Paul John Frandsen, Ole Herslund and Jens Jørgensen for reading drafts of this paper and for stimulating comments and discussions.

[1] For this trend within archaeology, see e.g. the recent reviews by L. Meskell, "Object Orientations", in: L. Meskell (ed.), *Archaeologies of Materiality*, Malden-Oxford-Carlton 2005, pp. 1-7 and R.A. Joyce, "Archaeology of the Body", *Annual Review of Anthropology* 34 (2005), pp. 139-158.

[2] E.g. R.W. Gibbs, "Embodied Experience and Linguistic Meaning", *Brain and Language* 84 (2003), pp. 1-15; L. Barsalou, P.M. Niedenthal, A.K. Barbey and J.A. Ruppert, "Social Embodiment", *The Psychology of Learning and Motivation* 43 (2003), pp. 43-92.

[3] M. Merleau-Ponty, *Phénoménologie de la perception*, Paris 1945, p. 225.

After a brief review of some central concepts in Schmitz's phenomenology, I will attempt to illustrate the usability of this approach by examining some ancient Egyptian linguistic expressions pertaining to the heart in order to elucidate the embodied experiences they describe.

1. The body in the "New Phenomenology" of Hermann Schmitz

One of the traditional philosophical views towards which phenomenology directs the most severe criticism is that of anthropological dualism, according to which human beings consist of two ontologically different and incommensurable parts, one physical (the body), and one psychological or mental (mind, soul, psyche etc.).[4] Not only is the interplay between these parts problematic, as illustrated by the so-called mind-body problem dealing with the question of how a physical substance can interact with a non-physical one, but in anthropology and related disciplines, it also causes great difficulties for the study of cultures that do not share this dichotomy.[5]

As part of his criticism of anthropological dualism and in an attempt to overcome the problems inherent in this view, Schmitz introduces a specific version of the non-dualistic phenomenological view of the body. At the core of this view lies the phenomenological distinction between two basic but very different ways of experiencing the human body. The first is the aspect expressed in German philosophy with the word *Körper*, designating the body as seen from outside as an object accessible to the senses in an objective way. The opposite view, and the one of particular importance to the phenomenological approach, is the body as experienced by the individual as seat of sensations, emotions etc., in short: *being-in-the-world*. In the German phenomenological tradition, the body seen in this way is designated *Leib*. In Hermann Schmitz's formulation of this distinction, *Körper* and *Leib* are defined according to their spatial characteristics,[6] which means that they are not mutually exclusive, but rather form two ends of a scale, in the middle of which is found what he terms *körperlicher Leib*:

> Der reine Leib ist bloß absolut-örtlich und gar nicht relativ-örtlich bestimmt; er kommt bei den panischen Zuständen von Angst, Schmerz und Wollust vor, wenn die räumliche Orientierung verloren gegangen ist. Der reine Körper ist bloß relativ-örtlich und gar nicht absolut-örtlich bestimmt; er bildet das Objekt der naturwissenschaftlichen Beschäftigung von Anatomie, Physiologie und exakt messender Medizin mit dem menschlichen Körper. In der Mitte zwischen Beiden steht der körperliche Leib, der sowohl absolut-örtlich als auch relativ-örtlich ist: das Gewoge verschwommener Inseln, die ebenso je für

[4] In Schmitz's analysis, this view consists of the more specific elements of *psychologism*, *reductionism* and *introjection*, cf. the succinct overview in H. Schmitz, "The 'New Phenomenology'", in: A.-T. Tymieniecka (ed.), *Phenomenology World-wide. Foundations - Expanding Dynamics - Life-Engagements, A Guide for Research and Study* (=Analecta Husserliana 80), Dordrecht 2003, p. 492.

[5] In the case of ancient Egypt, cf. e.g. R.B. Finnestad, "On transposing *Soul* and *Body* into a monistic conception of *Being*. An example from Ancient Egypt", *Religion* 16 (1986), pp. 359-373.

[6] The *Körper* is characterized by relative spatiality, meaning that, like other objects, the *Körper* or its parts are determined by spatial orientation, while the *Leib* is not dependent on or identified by spatial orientation (Schmitz, *Leib*, p. 5f). This distinction is very similar to one exemplified less formally by M. Merleau-Ponty: "Si mon bras est posé sur la table, je ne songerai jamais à dire qu'il est *à côté* du cendrier comme le cendrier est à côté du téléphone. Le contour de mon corps est une frontière que les relations d'espace ordinaires ne franchissent pas. C'est que les parties se rapportent les une aux autre d'une manière originale : elles ne sont pas déployées les une à côté des autres, mais enveloppées les unes dans les autres", *Phénoménologie de la perception*, p. 114, emphasis in original.

> sich einen relativen und einen absoluten Ort haben, wie sie durch einen absoluten Ort zur Einheit des Leibes im Ganzen zusammengehalten werden.[7]

Apart from this formal definition, an important difference between the two perspectives on the body is the way in which they are perceived. The *Körper* is accessible to the senses like other objects, it can be seen, touched etc. In contrast, the *Leib* is felt immediately without the use of the senses. However, it is also possible, both for oneself and for others, to experience parts of one's own body with the senses, and it follows from this that one's own body is most often experienced as a combination of *Körper* and *Leib*, in other words as *körperlicher Leib*. Schmitz illustrates the structural differences between the *Körper* and the *Leib* by means of a thought experiment:[8] Whereas the *Körper* is perceived as a whole when touched or viewed, the *Leib* is experienced as discrete, consisting of zones which can change both in size and number in different situations. This phenomenon is described by Schmitz in the central metaphor also found in the quote given above as "ein unstetiges Gewoge verschwommener Inseln"[9], and he accordingly terms these discrete, but ever changeable parts of the felt body (*Leib*)[10] as *Leibesinseln*. The basic notion in this metaphor is that the "islands" can change size, sometimes even disappear or join together under different influences such as pain or tickling, rather in the manner of dry land appearing and disappearing with changing tides. This labile structure of the felt body (*Leib*) and its parts is characterized by two basic polarities, namely that of narrowness (*Enge*) and expanse (*Weite*) on the one hand and the somewhat related, but independent polarity of protopathic and epicritic tendencies.

Narrowness is found in experiences where the islands of the felt body (*Leibesinseln*) are contracting and becoming small and tight, especially characteristic of feelings of fear and pain, while expanse is the opposite tendency of opening and projecting outwards. A simple illustration[11] can be found in the feeling of drawing breath in the chest and/or abdominal area, which begins with expanding of the island, and subsequently, towards the end of the inwards breathing, becoming a feeling of narrowness. This example also shows an important characteristic of the two poles, namely their cyclical or competitive interplay within individual islands or of the felt body as a whole, a phenomenon covered in Schmitz's notion of *leibliche Ökonomie*. Thus, most often a particular island is found somewhere in between the two extremes, only such intense emotions as deep panic or all-encompassing ecstasy being experiences of the actual poles of the continuum. Thus, the designations of the movement between these poles, *narrowing* and *expansion*, will prove to be of even greater use in the practical analysis. Often, both of these two tendencies will be at work at the same time, which may have various results depending on which of them is stronger in a given case. When narrowing and expansion are thus counteracting each other, the resulting process is known as tightening (*Spannung*) when it results in narrowing and swelling (*Schwellung*) when it results in expansion.

The notions of the epicritic and protopathic tendencies are defined succinctly by Schmitz in the following way: "Epikritisch ist die ortsfindende, protopathisch die Ortsfindung entgegenwirkende leibliche Tendenz."[12] A good example of this difference can be found in experiences of pain, where sharp pain is characterized by the epicritic tendency, whereas a dull,

[7] H. Schmitz, *Der Leib* (=System der Philosophie II/1), Bonn 1965, p. 54 (the quotations in this article are taken from the 2005 "Studienausgabe").
[8] Schmitz, *Leib*, p. 25f.
[9] Ibid., p. 28.
[10] The English translation of this and other key terms in Schmitz's philosophical system have been taken from the brief English overview in H. Schmitz, in: Tymieniecka (ed.), *Phenomenology World-wide*, pp. 491-494.
[11] Taken from H. Schmitz, *Der Leib, der Raum und die Gefühle*, Bielefeld and Locarno 2007, p. 16.
[12] Schmitz, *Leib*, p. 143.

thumping pain is protopathic. This dichotomy actually intersects that of narrowness and expanse, but at the same time, the epicritic tendency is often found in connection with that of narrowness (or indicates an undercurrent of narrowing in an experience characterized primarily by expanse), and likewise, expanse and the protopathic tendency are often experienced in conjunction.

These two polarities and the designations of processes taking place between them only form the core skeleton of what Schmitz terms the *Alphabet der Leibligkeit.* For the present purposes, these two important basic dichotomies will suffice, but it should be noted that Schmitz's terminology includes a number of more specific concepts relating to the interplay between the poles.[13] The combination of the two polarities may be illustrated in the following way:

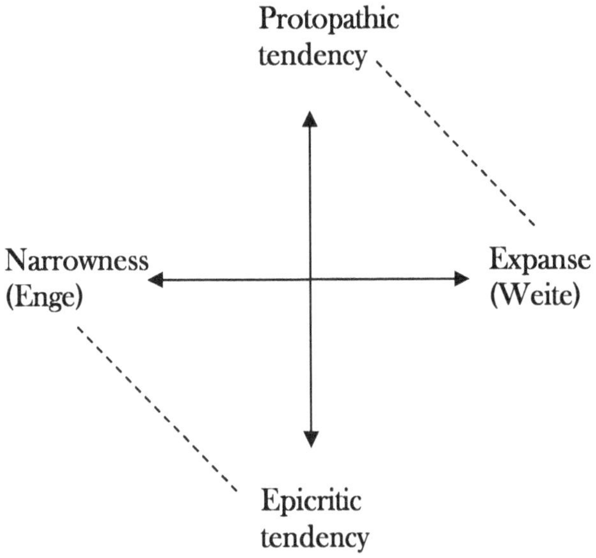

Fig. 1: The two polarities of *Leibliche Regungen* as understood by Hermann Schmitz

This theoretical background gives some important basic categories of use in identifying and classifying embodied experience. In relation to the main question posed here, namely that of the possibilities of connecting phenomenology and philology, these categories and the detailed analyses for which Schmitz employs them in his own work are of great relevance in the development of a methodology:

> Es kann nämlich der Fall eintreten, daß dem modernen Erleben Anschauungsbereiche zugänglich sind, die bloß in der modernen gewachsenen Sprache nicht verarbeitet werden, weil sie vergessen, verdrängt oder noch gar nicht bemerkt worden sind. Der Phänomenologe kann solche Bezirke aufdecken und im Hinblick auf die darin zu Tage tretenden Phänomene das Vokabular der gewachsenen Sprache in geeigneter Weise ergänzen. Dann kann sich herausstellen, daß diese zunächst in unhistorischer Einstellung zu Tage geförderten Phänomene gerade den Anschauungsboden liefern, den die Sprache des fremden Textes voraussetzt, die eigene des Philologen aber anfangs nicht nachzubilden vermochte.[14]

In this way, the *Alphabet der Leiblichkeit* developed by Schmitz offers an expansion of the analytical vocabulary available to the modern philologist, which makes it possible to sophisticate and expand philological analyses of texts dealing with ancient Egyptian embodied experiences.

[13] See Schmitz, *Leib*, pp. 169-172 for an overview.
[14] Schmitz, *Der Leib*, p. 368f.

2. Ancient Egyptian conceptions of the heart in a phenomenological perspective

It is a well-known Egyptological convention that the Egyptian language had two synonyms referring to the heart, namely *ib*, usually regarded as the older term and connected to Semitic √*lb*, and *ḥ3ty*, which is the term that ends up winning the terminological "competition" and being the only designation of the heart to survive in the Coptic stage of the language.[15] The phenomenological perspective taken here suggests a few changes to this view, though the main point of this paper is not to discuss this question in any detail. Thus, the fact alone that the usage of the two terms exhibits important and consistent differences indicates that they should initially be treated apart as separate islands of the felt body (*Leibesinseln*).[16] In other words, one would expect *a priori* that the reason why expressions with *ib* and *ḥ3ty* could be originally held apart in the Egyptian conceptualization is that they referred to different islands of the felt body and thus to different bodily experiences - which does not necessarily exclude that a more reductionistic biomedical viewpoint would associate them with the same *Körper*-organ.[17] It should be noted, however, that in the course of the language development that would eventually lead to the disappearance of *ib* and the predominance of *ḥ3ty*, the latter term gradually encroached upon the territory originally being covered by the former. This is especially clear from the New Kingdom onwards, while the original distinction seems to hold to a large extent throughout the Old and Middle Kingdoms.[18]

Rather than revisiting the question of the similarities and differences between the two terms, however, I would like to take a different point of departure here in order to exemplify the usability of the phenomenological perspective. In the case of the term *ḥ3ty*, there is widespread agreement, for reasons that will be detailed below, that the term refers centrally to the physical heart as part of the *Körper*. At the same time, however, already in the Old Kingdom, the term was used to describe emotions and experiences in ways that clearly point towards an understanding of the term as designating a part of the felt body. This combination of usages makes the term *ḥ3ty* very well-suited as an example of a phenomenological perspective on the body.

2.1 The ḥ3ty as part of an (animal) Körper

This is the main usage of the term in the Old Kingdom, and remains of great importance throughout the Middle Kingdom as well. The clearest examples of this use of the term are found in the phraseology of captions to depictions of butchery in Old Kingdom tomb scenes. The basic expression for the removal of the heart from the carcass is *šdi ḥ3ty*, "taking out the heart"[19], but such scene captions offer a further range of objectifying expressions in which the

---

[15] For a summary of this conventional view, see W. Westendorf, *Handbuch der altägyptischen Medizin* (=HdO II/36), Leiden-Boston-Cologne 1999, vol. I, p. 108f.

[16] For a way to characterize the differences between the two terms formally, as well as a discussion of the relevance of these differences, see R. Nyord, *Breathing Flesh. Conceptions of the body in the ancient Egyptian Coffin Texts*, (=CNI Publications 37), Copenhagen, forthcoming, section 2.4.

[17] Cf. e.g. the similar case with the several ancient Greek heart terms discussed in Schmitz, *Leib*, pp. 426-436. In the discussion cited in the previous note, I tentatively suggested that the usage of the Egyptian terms might be more easily accounted for by assuming that the two terms refer to different areas of the torso, but I know of no certain examples that might be used as conclusive evidence either way.

[18] Thus, apart from the very few instances to be discussed below, all occurrences of metaphors with the word *ḥ3ty* are of New Kingdom date in the convenient collection of "heart" metaphors in wisdom literature, love songs and narratives of the 2nd millennium BC in M.I. Toro Rueda, *Das Herz in der ägyptischen Literatur des zweiten Jarhtausends v. Chr. Untersuchungen zu Idiomatik und Metaphorik von Audrücken mit jb und ḥ3tj*, dissertation Göttingen 2003, pp. 335-347.

[19] *Wb.* III, 27, 7; R. Hannig, *Ägyptisches Wörterbuch I. Altes Reich und Erste Zwischenzeit* (=Kultugeschichte der antike Welt 98), Mainz am Rhein 2003, p. 766f (no. 19541). E.g. S. Hassan, *Excavations at Gîza 1930-1931*, vol. 2, Cairo 1936, p. 118, fig. 127; id., *Excavations at Gîza 1934-1935*, vol. 6/3, Cairo 1950, p. 115, fig. 101; id.,

heart is clearly conceptualized as an object susceptible to physical manipulations, including being "given" (*rḏi*, imperative *imi*),[20] and "taken"(*iṯi*).[21]

The basic conceptual structure of these examples is that the body of the ox constitutes a CONTAINER[22] from which the heart can be "taken out" (*šdi*) or "caused to exit" (*rdi pri*),[23] and the expressions with their accompanying depictions make it clear that when the heart of an animal was referred to as a piece of meat in a butchering context, the word *ḥ3ty* was used.[24] This usage of the term is also the most prominent of the roles of the heart in the Pyramid Texts.[25]

2.2 The ḥ3ty as an island of Leib[26]

An interpretation which chooses to emphasize only examples like those mentioned above – clear as they may be – of the conceptualization of the heart encounters problems with other passages of the Pyramid Texts where the heart occurs clearly as a locus of experiences in the lived body (i.e. as a *Leibesinsel*), though as it happens such examples are only found from the pyramid of Teti onwards. These early occurrences are important because they show that this usage was part of the central meaning of the word *ḥ3ty* from early on in the written history of the term, and for this reason should be briefly reviewed. After discussing the evidence from the Pyramid Texts, the examples from Middle Kingdom literary texts will be considered in order to

---

Excavations at Saqqara, 1937-1938, vol. 1, Cairo 1975, p. 19 fig. 4; W. K. Simpson, *The Offering Chapel of Sekhem-Ankh-Ptah in the Museum of Fine Arts, Boston*, Boston 1976, plate IIb (photo), p. 5 fig. 2 (line drawing); A.M. Moussa and H. Altenmüller: *Das Grab des Nianchchnum und Chnumhotep* (=Archäologische Veröffentlichungen 21), Mainz 1977, pl. 86, lower register; A. M. Roth, *A Cemetery of Palace Attendants, Including G 2084-2099, G 2230+2231, and G 2240* (=Giza Mastabas 6), Boston 1995, pl. 178. A discussion of these scenes with further examples is found in A. Eggebrecht, *Schlachtungsbräuche im alten Ägypten und ihre Wiedergabe im Flachbild bis zum Ende des mittleren Reiches*, Munich 1963, pp. 79-87.

[20] E.g. A. Badawy, *The Tomb of Nyhetep-Ptah at Giza and the Tomb of 'Ankhm'ahor at Saqqara*, Berkeley-Los Angeles-London 1978, pl. 61 (photo) = N. Kanawati and A. Hassan, *The Teti Cemetery at Saqqara II: The Tomb of Ankhmahor* (=ACE Reports 9), Warminster 1997, pl. 49 (line drawing), middle register, 2nd scene from the right; H. Altenmüller, *Die Wanddarstellung im Grab des Mehu in Saqqara*, (=Archäologische Veröffentlichungen 42), Mainz 1998, pl. 73. Further exx. in P. Montet, *Les scenes de la vie privée dans les tombeaux égyptiens de l'Ancien Empire*, Strassbourg and Paris 1925, p. 173f.

[21] Two examples are found in N. Kanawati, M. Abder-Raziq, *The Teti Cemetery at Saqqara VI: The Tomb of Nikauisesi* (=ACE Rep. 14), Warminster 2000, 48-50, pl. 30 (photo) and 61 (line drawing), one reading *iṯ ḥ3ty sin*, "Take the heart quickly!", and the other *mk ḥ3ty iṯ sw*, "Look, the heart, take it!" (for the first part of this expression, cf. J.E. Quibbel, *The Ramesseum and the Tomb of Ptahshepses*, London 1898, pl. 36, lower register, *mk ḥ3ty pn*, "Look at this heart").

[22] Understood as an image schema in the sense of M. Johnson, *The body in the mind. The bodily basis of meaning, imagination, and reason*, Chicago and London 1987, pp. 21-23.

[23] Kanawati, Naguib, *The rock tombs of El-Hawawish. The cemetery of Akhmim 2*, Sydney 1981, fig. 26, upper register.

[24] Also noted by Eggebrecht, *Schlachtungsbräuche*, p. 79 n. 1. Since the great majority of the cases have the designation of the heart written clearly as *ḥ3ty*, it seems methodically preferable to follow A.H. Gardiner, *Ancient Egyptian Onomastica*, Oxford 1947, vol. 2, p. 251* in assuming that the rare examples of the abbreviated writing 𓄣 in butchery scenes is still, exceptionally, to be read in this way, which also seems to have been the general practice since Gardiner's remarks, e.g. Simpson, *Sekhem-Ankh-Ptah*, p. 6. As possible reasons for such an exceptional usage may be mentioned (1) the generally very economic use of signs in scene captions due to space constraints, and (2) the clear context which meant that even when written similarly to a different word, the term was highly unlikely to be misunderstood (cf. the similar cases mentioned by E. Edel, *Altägyptische Grammatik*, vol. I (=Analecta Orientalia 34), Rome 1955, p. 23f).

[25] See Nyord, *Breathing Flesh*, nn. 710-711 for the attestations.

[26] A third group, which will not be dealt with here, consists of expressions of the metaphorical qualities of the heart without apparently dealing directly with embodied experiences, most notably laudatory epithets such as *mtr ḥ3ty* (e.g. F.L. Griffith, *The Inscriptions of Siut and Deir Rifeh*, London 1889, pl. 4, l. 220) and *ʿq3 ḥ3ty* (e.g. ibid., pl. 19, l. 46), "precision of heart". The epithet *dšr ḥ3ty*, "redness of heart" (C. Barbotin and J.J. Clère, "L'inscription de Sesostris Ier à Tôd", *BIFAO* 91 (1991), fig. 3, l. 32) in a war context might belong in this group as well, or it might be a conceptualization of a particular embodied experience. With only one example, occurring immediately after a lacuna, it seems impossible at the present to elucidate this question.

complete the examination of expressions referring to the heart as a *Leibesinsel* in the Old and Middle Kingdom.[27] The literary evidence has the advantage of presenting situations which are often much more detailed and hence easier to understand and evaluate than those found in the mortuary literature.

2.2.1. The Pyramid Texts

Clear examples of references to the heart as a part of the *Leib* are found in the Pyramid Texts, when the heart is mentioned as the part of the body of enemies influenced by the fear of the deceased,[28] and in a passage which should certainly be understood metaphorically, where Horus is said to have placed the deceased in the hearts of the gods.[29] Though the exact relevance of the latter action is not clear from the passage, this notion may be connected with another metaphorical use where it said that the deceased in his turn loves (*mri*) Re in his belly and in his heart.[30]

A few further Pyramid Texts examples refer to particular states of this island of the felt body. Thus, the goddess Qebehet is said to purify the deceased and the sun god when they manifest together in the sky: "This N finds Qebehet, the daughter of Anubis, having come to meet him with those four *nmst*-jars of hers. When cooling (*sqbḥ*) the heart of the Great God therewith on his day of awakening, she cools the heart of this N for him therewith for life, purifying (*wʿb*) this N and censing (*snṯr*) this N."[31] The context here is the awakening and subsequent purification of the deceased to prepare him for receiving offerings, and the important element of the passage does not appear so much to be the specific body part as the act of *sqbḥ*, a root occurring repeatedly in the passage. That *qbḥ ḥꜣty* is not likely to be a fixed metaphor finds further support in the fact that the slightly more detailed parallel from the pyramid of Pepi I reads "she cools (*sqbḥ*) and freshens (*sḫn*) your interior (*ib*)[32] inside your belly",[33] so that the main concern seems to be the cooling of an internal body part, be it heart (*ḥꜣty*) or interior (*ib*). From the distribution of the root (which includes references to libation offerings[34] and a cataract area[35]), it would seem that the prototype of the word *qbḥ* is cool, fresh, running water, and as such, the libation becomes a very suitable metaphor for the swelling experience of vigour,[36] applicable to either of the two important *Leibesinseln* of the torso.[37]

---

[27] This paper does not discuss the Coffin Texts examples, as these have been dealt with in detail by the present author in Nyord, *Breathing Flesh*, chapter 2.

[28] *Pyr.* 763b (*snḏ*); 763d (*šʿt*) [422]. Similarly in later texts, *CT* I, 78c [26]; VII, 16p [817] (both with *šfšft*); *pMoscow Pushkin* 314, 19, 4 (=A. Erman, *Hymnen an das Diadem der Pharaonen aus einem Papyrus der Sammlung Golenischeff*, Berlin 1911, p. 52) (*šʿt*).

[29] *Pyr.* 648a [371]. Such expressions are much more frequent with the interior (*ib*, cf. n 32 below for this translation) or the belly (*ẖt*), but cf. e.g. the 18th Dynasty autobiographical inscription of Nefer (A. Gaballa, "Nufer, third prophet of Amon", *MDAIK* 26 (1970), p. 53 fig. 1, right side, l. 1-2), *di=i nṯr=i m ib=i nsw m ḥꜣty=i šfšft nt nb=i ẖt ʿwt=i* , "I placed my god in my interior, the king in my heart, and the awe of my lord throughout my body parts", where the phrases are clearly parallel expressions of loyalty and devotion.

[30] *Pyr.* 1442d [569].

[31] *Pyr.* 1180b-1181b [515].

[32] This translation is adapted from the "intérieur-*ib*" of T. Bardinet, *Les papyrus médicaux de l'Égypte pharaonique*, Paris 1995, pp. 68ff, primarily in order to keep it clearly distinct from the term *ḥꜣty*, "heart", under discussion here. For a detailed presentation of the similarities and differences between the two terms, see the reference cited in n. 16 above.

[33] J. Leclant, *Les textes de la pyramide de Pépy Ier* (=MIFAO 118), Cairo 2001, pl. 6, l. 4 ; similarly *Pyr.* 1995b [673] = G. Jéquier, *Les pyramides des reines Neit et Apouit*, Cairo 1933, pl. 22, l. 603.

[34] *Wb.* V, 26-28.

[35] *Wb.* V, 29, 5-6.

[36] Cf. the similar expressions found in the Schiller poem analyzed by Schmitz, *Leib*, p. 246: "Das Wallen der Jugend, das Schäumen des Lebens sind Metaphern für Schwellung des Leibes, da wallende, schäumende Flüssigkeit kraftvoll anschwillt. Schwellung ist eine Weise leiblicher Weitung; diese wird hier auch noch als Lüften der Brust dargestellt".

A different metaphorical expression is found when, in the context of the enthronement of the deceased in *PT* 677, it is said, "May your interior be sweet (*nḏm ỉb=k*) , and may your heart be great (*ꜥ3 ḥ3ty=k*)!"[38] The context is that of the bodily reconstitution of the deceased, but it is very unlikely that the two expressions should be read as descriptions of the physical properties of organs of the *Körper*. Indeed, the expression *nḏm ỉb* is well-attested as an expression of joy, especially as felt following a successful accomplishment.[39] On the other hand, *ꜥ3 ḥ3ty* is very rare in the period under discussion here,[40] but in later times, the expression seems to refer mainly to the ability to remain calm or become reassured under adverse circumstances.[41] These examples, as well as the fact that the expression is found in the *PT* passage in the form of an exhortation, shows that we cannot be dealing simply with the size of a *Körper* organ. Thus, from the root meaning of the expression, it can be seen that we are dealing again with an expression falling under the heading of expansion (*Weitung*) in the terminology of Schmitz. The expression may then be understood as one of swelling joy in parallel with the expression *nḏm ỉb*, or more precisely (in light of the later evidence) as the ability to withstand the tightening feeling of circumstances that cause fear or anxiety. This experience is at once characterized by swelling, i.e. expansion overriding a feeling of narrowing, and by the epicritic tendency accompanying that narrowing and localizing the experience to this particular island of the felt body.

Such examples show that from early on in the Egyptian history, the heart could in fact be conceptualized as a part of the lived body which makes itself felt in relation to experiences of fear, love (in the context of *PT* 569 clearly, and perhaps also in *PT* 371 connected to the family relation between the deceased and the gods) and keeping one's spirits high (*PT* 677), and not only as a reference to the heart viewed in an objectifying manner from outside the body in which it resides.

2.2.2. Middle Kingdom Literary Texts

The extreme paucity of such examples is a trend which continues into the Middle Kingdom, and not until the gradual disappearance of the "competing" term *ỉb* (outside the most traditional texts) during the New Kingdom does this picture begin to change.[42]

The first clear literary example to be examined here of the use of the term *ḥ3ty* as referring to an island of the felt body is found in two parallel passages in the Middle Kingdom story of *Sinuhe* in which the protagonist is under the influence of extreme emotional turmoil, first as a reaction to news of the death of the old king, which – as Sinuhe himself relates the events – cause him to flee the country, and again when Sinuhe much later returns to Egypt and is brought before the new king whose majestic presence overwhelms the protagonist:

> "My interior (*ỉb*) grew weak,[43] and as for my heart, it was not even[44] in my torso, and on the ways of flight it brought me." (*Sinuhe* B38-40)[45]

---

[37] Note also the related lexicalized use of the phrase *qbb ỉb*, "cool of interior", for which cf. Nyord, *Breathing Flesh*, section 2.3.1.2.

[38] *Pyr.* 2024a [677].

[39] Nyord, *Breathing Flesh*, section 2.3.1.9.

[40] Hannig, *Wörterbuch I*, p. 767 (no. 19561) cites only this example.

[41] As evidenced by the examples collected by G.R. Hughes, "A Demotic Letter to Thoth", *JNES* 17 (1958), p. 9f, to which may be added *Qadesh Poem* §245 = *KRI* II, 77, 1-4 where the expression is found as a laudatory epithet to the king. Cf. further W. Helck, "Eine Briefsammlung aus der Verwaltung des Amuntempels", *JARCE* 6 (1967), p. 136 n. h, and the use of the expression in Late Egyptian letters of the reassuring effect of receiving news from the correspondent, e.g. *LRL* 24, 4; 28, 9; 34,4; a slightly different phraseology is found ibid., 3,15.

[42] Cf. n. 18 above.

[43] Reading *3hd* here and in B255, following Gardiner, *Notes on Sinuhe*, p. 30. The B MS. has the verb *3d* in both cases, and AOS reads *h3mw*, "suffering".

> "I was like a man caught in the twilight, my *ba* being perished, my body (*ḥʿ*) weak, and as for my heart, it was not even in my torso. I did <not> know life from death." (*Sinuhe* B254-256)[46]

In these descriptions, a number of body parts and aspects of the personality are enumerated, each with their own particular experience of deficiency. In both descriptions, the expression dealing with the state of the heart is paralleled with the state of *3hd*, "weakness"[47] in other body parts, namely the interior (*ib*) and the body (*ḥʿ*), and, as V. Tobin has remarked, the absence of the heart constitutes "a graphic description of panic".[48] In the phenomenological terminology of Schmitz, the absence of a part of the felt body is referred to as "Leibinselschwund bei gesteigerter Spannung".[49] In direct contrast to the experience of the heart being great (*ʿ3 ḥ3ty*) discussed above, in this case the experience is one of extreme tightening to the point where the heart is felt as being absent.[50] In the two *Sinuhe* passages, the loss of the heart is experienced in conjunction with weakness or fatigue, a feeling typically characterized by a protopathic tendency.[51] The combination of this experience with that of having lost the heart as a result of tightening describes a very particular bodily experience, in which the tightening sensation is split up by the protopathic tendency, causing a feeling of complete exhaustion, expressed in the second passage quoted as "not knowing life from death".[52] In the first passage, the effect is slightly different, as the heart is said there to cause Sinuhe's flight, presumably due to its absence described in the preceding clause.[53] This somewhat odd notion can also be made sensible in the light of phenomenology. As mentioned, the loss of the experience of a part of the lived body as described in the *Sinuhe* passage is due to an extreme fear-induced tightening, which according to the *leibliche Ökonomie* as defined by Hermann Schmitz, is invariably countered by a swelling impulse to flee,[54] an impulse upon which Sinuhe instinctively acts in this passage.

---

[44] Following M. Gilula, "Sinuhe B 255", *JNES* 35 (1976), pp. 25-28 in understanding the use of the independent pronoun here as due to a shift of emphasis. Cf. also J.P. Allen, "Pronominal Rhematization", in: D.P. Silverman (ed.), *For His Ka. Essays offered in memory of Klaus Baer* (=SAOC 55), Chicago 1994, p. 8 n. 18. Note that the focalizing construction, if correctly understood, would be among the clearest indications that *ib* and *ḥ3ty* were still understood as separate parts of the body at his point.

[45] R. Koch, *Die Erzählung des Sinuhe* (=BiAeg 17), Bruxelles 1990, p. 28.

[46] Koch, *Sinuhe*, p. 73-74.

[47] Cf. n. 43 above for the variants.

[48] V.A. Tobin, "The Secret of Sinuhe", *JARCE* 32 (1995), p. 172 n. 49.

[49] Schmitz, *Leib*, p. 164-169.

[50] Ibid., p. 165: "In diesem Fall gewinnt die von der Spannung aufrecht erhaltene Einheit des Leibes ein Übergewicht, das die Leibesinseln wenig zu selbständiger Entfaltung gelangen und eventuell – bei sehr starker und übermäßiger Spannung – teilweise in der Einheit des Leibes verschwinden läßt"; a similar analysis is offered at id., "Leibliche Quellen der Herzmetaphorik", in: G. Berkemer and G. Rappe (eds.), *Das Herz im Kulturvergleich* (=Lynkeus. Studien zur Neuen Phänomenologie 3), Berlin 1996, p. 19f.

[51] Schmitz, *Leib*, p. 251, defines "Müdigkeit" as "Überschwemmung des Leibes durch protopathische Tendenz unter Lockerung des Bandes der leiblichen Ökonomie, wobei Spannung abgespalten und das Richten gestört wird".

[52] Schmitz, *Leib*, p. 251, "Wenn [...] die Abspaltung der Spannung im Wesentlichen bloß ihre Aufsplitterung in irrlichthafte Partialspannungen erreicht [...], dann kommt es zu der unruhigen, mißmutigen, erschöpften, zerstreuten Müdigkeit dessen, der sich 'wie zerschlagen' oder gar 'wie gerädert' fühlt."

[53] Compare also the discussion of the passage in R. Parant, *L'affaire Sinouhé. Tentative d'approche de la justice repressive égyptienne au début du IIe millénaire av. J.C.*, Aurillac 1982, pp. 129-131, where a few further examples of similar expressions are given.

[54] Schmitz, *Leib*, p. 122: "Die Angst liefert auch ein anschauliches Beispiel für das beständige Auf und Ab von Spannung und Schwellung trotz beharrlichen Übergewichts des einen von beiden Impulsen (hier der Spannung): Immer wieder bäumt sich das schwellende 'Weg!' gegen die Hemmung auf, immer wieder wird es zurückgeworfen von der in der Angst beständig übermächtigen Spannung als der Einengung, die den Impuls 'Weg!' am Durchbruch hindert und nicht zur Ruhe kommen läßt, indem sie ihn in rhythmischen Pulsen desto mehr aufstachelt, je stärker sie ihn zurückhält und seinen Erfolg vereitelt."

In connection with this highly elaborate and precise description of bodily experiences, it is quite interesting that one of the very few unequivocal references in Egyptian texts to the *ba* of a living person[55] occurs precisely in such a phenomenologically charged passage. While a more detailed examination of the question falls outside the scope of this paper, it would appear that whatever an Egyptian *ba* may be,[56] its absence makes itself felt in equal measure to the loss in *Sinuhe* of the feeling of the heart, and so it is tempting to consider whether the presence and activities of the *ba* as known from elsewhere could also to some extent be regarded as a description of phenomenological experiences (as opposed e.g. to being the result of theological speculation), a question which can only be answered by making a detailed phenomenological re-examination of the evidence.

A few final examples of the use of the term *ḥ3ty* to conceptualize embodied experience should be mentioned to exemplify additional combinations of the polarities of narrowness vs. expanse and epicritic vs. protopathic tendencies. The first example is found again in the story of Sinuhe. At the approach of the warrior who wishes to fight Sinuhe, the people around him react with anxiety:

> "Every heart was kindled for me, the wives were chattering anxiously(?), every interior (*ỉb*) being painful for me, saying 'Is there another warrior who can fight him?'" (*Sinuhe* B131-134)

In this passage, a clear parallelism is found between the phrase *ḥ3ty m3ẖ*, "the heart is kindled" and the much more frequently attested *mr ỉb n*, "the interior is painful for..." as an expression of empathy or feeling sorry for someone.[57] This parallelism with *mr* forms the basis of all previous attempts to translate the unique expression, but in the present perspective it also shows that we should understand the experience of fire here as the "unerträglich fressendes Feuer"[58] characteristic of the feeling of narrowness resulting from fear or pain, here said to be located in the heart. Again, quite opposite the feeling of comfort expressed as the heart being large (*ʿ3 ḥ3ty*), not only is the heart here sore from narrowness caused by the anxiety that Sinuhe might come to harm, but a veritable burning makes itself felt epicritically in the heart, causing the bystanders to attempt to find some other way out of the predicament.[59]

A final example goes to show the range of possible situations in which the heart can make itself felt by introducing the description of an experience which has both similarities and differences with some of those discussed above. In the *Teaching of Amenemhet*, the king describes how he falls into a deep slumber after having gone to bed, a description which refers to the heart in the following terms:

> "I lay down on my bed and I became fatigued as soon as my heart had started to follow my sleep" (*Amenemhat* §6c-d, pMillingen)[60]

---

[55] Cf. L.V. Žabkar, *A Study of the Ba Concept in Ancient Egyptian Texts* (=SAOC 34), Chicago 1968, p. 119, where it is suggested that such examples "might be anticipatory of the coming into existence of the Ba at death and somewhat analogous to our expressions 'he almost died of fear' or 'he was scared to death'". This, however, does not really fit with what the wording of the text seems to presuppose, so a phenomenological re-examination like the one suggested here seems to be worthwhile. For the role of the *ba* in the *Sinuhe* passage, see most recently E. Meyer-Dietrich, *Senebi und Selbst. Personenkonstituenten zur rituellen Wiedergeburt in einem Frauensarg des Mittleren Reiches* (=OBO 216), Freibourg and Göttingen 2006, pp. 326f and 334f.

[56] Cf. also the discussion by J. Gee in this volume.

[57] Cf. Nyord, *Breathing Flesh*, section 2.3.1.4 for this expression.

[58] Schmitz, *Leib*, p. 73.

[59] Cf. n. 54 above.

[60] F. Adrom, *Die Lehre des Amenemhet* (=BiAeg 19), Turnhout 2006, p. 38-39.

The meaning of the conceptualization of the process of falling asleep in this passage is to be sought in the root semantics of the verb *šms*, "follow". Being a verb of movement, the word signalizes that the basic situation is most probably one of the outward directionality of the island of the felt body, or in other words a case of expansion. At the same time, the heart is not only expanding, but it is doing so in what is conceptualized metaphorically as an act of "following" a particular state, namely sleep. Thus, in a manner completely opposite to the panic and exhaustion experienced by Sinuhe as discussed above, the sleeper in this passage is overcome by expansion, leaving him in a pleasant state of protopathic inertness.[61]

3. Conclusion

The expressions examined in the previous section may be localized in the figure showing the two polarities of the felt body as shown on Fig. 2.

Each of the four examples included in the figure illustrates a particular combination of the two polarities of narrowness vs. expanse and the epicritic vs. protopathic tendencies. The expression of not having the heart in one's torso (*m ẖt*) combines extreme narrowness with the protopathic tendency characteristic of exhaustion. The latter tendency is also found in the expression from the *Teaching of Amenemhet* of the heart following sleep (*šms ḥ3ty qd*), the difference lying in the notion of expansion inherent in the verb "follow", which points towards a different, much more pleasant type of tiredness leading to sleep. When the heart is described as great (*ˁ3 ḥ3ty*), the experience can be seen as the exact opposite to the loss of the heart in the upper left corner of the figure. Here, the heart swells in spite of a tendency towards narrowness, without losing the specific localization of this *Leibesinsel*, the experience thus being characterized by the epicritic tendency. This tendency is also found in the final example, the heart being kindled (*ḥ3ty m3ẖ*), illustrated at the lower left in the figure, in which the localizing tendency is combined with a painful, burning feeling of narrowing.

The examination summarized in the figure has shown on the one hand the somewhat limited distribution of expressions referring to the heart as an island of the felt body in the Old and Middle Kingdoms, as opposed to the much more numerous examples of the word as referring to an organ of the *Körper*. On the other hand, the discussion has also shown the way in which a detailed phenomenological analysis can be used to refine more traditional philological analyses which often lack the conceptual apparatus to go beyond a simple identification of a modern equivalent term or paraphrase which seems to fit the context. The schematic overview in the figure further illustrates that, although few in number, the attestations of expressions with *ḥ3ty* as part of the felt body actually cover the full spectrum of combinations of the two poles of embodied experience, which further stresses the fact that the role of the *ḥ3ty* as part of the felt body is far from negligible, however rare.

An important more general conclusion of the discussion is that it has proven perfectly possible to incorporate phenomenological aspects into ancient Egyptian philological research. By introducing a set of analytical terms from phenomenology for characterizing embodied experience, it becomes possible to reach a more nuanced understanding of the Egyptian expressions than purely traditional lexicographic methods allow.

---

[61] Cf. Schmitz, *Leib*, p. 83f and the passage from Nietzsche's *Also sprach Zarathustra* cited there, "Wie sie mir lang und müde wird, meine wunderliche Seele!", etc.

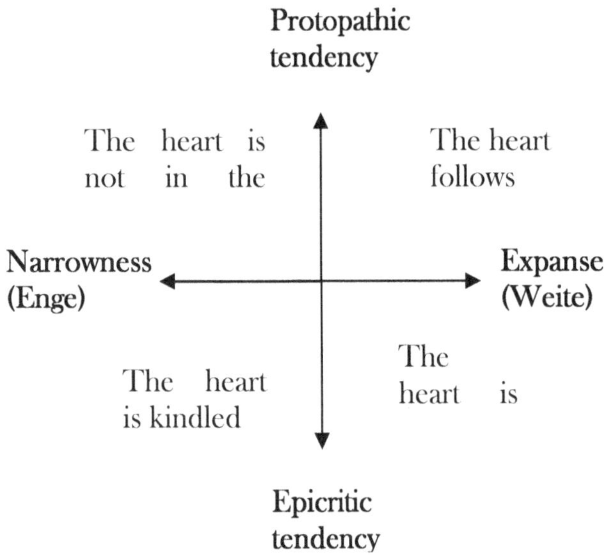

Fig. 2: The expressions dealing with the heart as part of the felt body

The avenue of approach exemplified here offers great promise for understanding aspects of embodiment in ancient Egyptian texts, and while the present study has confined itself to examples from religious and literary texts, a particularly promising material for phenomenological analyses is found in the numerous metaphorical expressions involving the body and its parts in the medical literature. In a phenomenological perspective like the one exemplified here, the analysis of such expressions would not so much be directed towards identifying modern equivalents to the illnesses, but instead focus on a reading of the expressions as conceptualizations of embodied experience.[62]

[62] Cf. also the criticism of the traditional approach in G. Rappe, *Archaische Leiberfahrung. Der Leib in der frühgriechischen Philosophie und in außereuropäischen Kulturen* (=Lynkeus. Studien zur Neuen Phänomenologie 2), Berlin 1995, pp. 279-281.

Anger and Agency

The role of the emotions in Demotic and earlier narratives*

John Tait

The aim of this contribution is to explore some of the uses of the concept of anger in Egyptian narrative texts. The starting point will be Demotic narratives, where the handling of anger is, arguably, rather consistent. The opportunity will then be taken to consider, very briefly, how far earlier Egyptian stories treat anger in the same way as Demotic. The aim is to throw light on the workings of Egyptian narrative structure and strategies, rather than upon the behaviour of ancient Egyptians. It may be legitimate in passing to comment here on the Egyptians' attitudes to anger, but even this must be recognised as hazardous.

Anger may be regarded as to all intents and purposes a human universal. We can reasonably assume that the psychological and physiological mechanisms of anger are common to all humans of the last few millennia. What clearly vary are the view a society may take of anger and the uses it may make of it—how it is exploited or controlled in social interactions. These matters can be very changeable. Some fifty years ago, it was quite acceptable for a schoolteacher in England to display a burst of anger in class, as long as this did not descend into verbal abuse or violence. Now it would be labelled as inappropriate behaviour. In present-day England, the acceptability of displays of anger varies in different social classes, and for example in different professional contexts: a kind of stylised anger is expected of professional boxers, and perhaps of politicians.

I am not aware of previous work quite along the same lines as what is attempted here. The studies of documentary and literary texts by Sweeney are highly relevant, especially her analysis of the New Kingdom *Horus and Seth* story.[1] There, however, she discusses anger chiefly in order to explore the different expectations of male and female behaviour that are revealed in the text, rather than as an aspect of narrative structure. In his discussion of the Demotic P. Krall, Hoffmann has pointed to 'Phrase(n) zur Einleitung von Erzählabschnitten' and includes phrases such as those considered here in examining how the narrative handles time and moves from one thread of the story to another.[2]

* I am most grateful to the organisers of the Copenhagen conference 'Being in Ancient Egypt' for the opportunity to present these ideas, and to participants for their helpful remarks. I also wish to thank the editors for their encouragement and valuable comments.

[1] Sweeney, D., 'Gender and Conversational Tactics in *The Contendings of Horus and Seth*', *JEA* 88 (2002), pp. 141-162.

[2] Hoffmann, F., *Der Kampf um den Panzer des Inaros. Studien zum P. Krall und seiner Stellung innerhalb des Inaros-Petubastis-Zyklus*, Wien 1996, p. 34; pp. 37-39; cf. Hoffmann, F., *Ägypter und Amazonen. Neubearbeitung zweier demotischer Papyri P. Vindob. D 6165 und P. Vindob. D 6165 A*, Wien 1995, p. 17, and Hoffmann, F. and Quack, J.F., *Anthologie der Demotischen Literatur* (Einführungen und Quellentexte zur Ägyptologie 4), Berlin 2007, p. 16.

JOHN TAIT

Structural Signposts: Key Phrases in Demotic Narrative

In Demotic narratives, anger and other emotions for the most part are not aspects of human behaviour that are just mentioned whenever they happen to arise in the unfolding of the action. Rather, they are usually referred to in recognisable expressions, with largely fixed phraseology; they occur in restricted types of context, and have a particular task to perform in signposting to the story's audience their pathway in following the narrative. In these respects, mentions of emotion behave in a very similar manner to a range of other key phrases.

The author has written elsewhere on the structural function of a number of such phrases or combinations of phrases that recur within and between Demotic narratives.[3] A typical brief example is

> *wꜥt wnw.t tꜣ ỉ-ir ḫpr*
> 'A moment that happened, ...', or perhaps 'Somewhat later, ...'.[4]

The context of this example is that the sun-god has granted the god Thoth's request that Naneferkaptah and his family may be punished for the theft of Thoth's magical book-roll. The phrase cited then introduces the account of the seemingly accidental drowning of Naneferkaptah's only son Merib. Although purely temporal in sense, the phrase, alone, marks the transition from cause (the sun-god's condemnation of Naneferkaptah) to effect (the first death of a member of Naneferkaptah's family), and a shift from the realm of deities to human events on earth.

A longer example is

> *tꜣ wnw.t n sḏy r-ỉr pꜣ wꜥb [n Nꜣ-nfr-kꜣ-Ptḥ] bn-pw=f gm mꜣꜥ nb n pꜣ tꜣ ỉw=f n-ỉm=f*
> 'The moment of the narration that the priest did [to Naneferkaptah], he did not find any place of the earth where he was', or 'Naneferkaptah was carried away by excitement, as soon as the priest had told him this'.[5]

These phrases follow Naneferkaptah's learning of the location of the hiding-place of Thoth's book, and introduce his impulsive decision to appropriate it.

Structural signposts most typically occur at the very beginning of a new 'episode'. They are not used so mechanically that they lose their straightforward literal meaning: for example, they do not occur in contexts where their literal meaning is inappropriate,[6] and some variation in the phraseology can be seen in and between texts. However, their structural roles include indicating a juncture in the narration: the beginning of a new stage in the story or a switch in the type of discourse, or a shift of register or tone. Most of them also serve to guide the audience in other but related ways, giving them an idea of what to expect next. Therefore a certain degree of standardisation in the phrases is absolutely necessary, so that their role and message may be recognised, albeit no doubt unconsciously.

---

[3] Tait, J., 'The Sinews of Demotic Narrative'. Forthcoming.

[4] *First Setna* 4/8 (Goldbrunner, S., *Der Verblendete Gelehrte. Der Erste Setna-Roman (P.Kairo 30646)* (Demotische Studien 13), Sommerhausen 2006).

[5] *First Setna* 3/20.

[6] It has often been pointed out that some instances of rather similar time expressions in the New Kingdom *Tale of the Two Brothers* make little sense: see for example Wente's translation of the opening paragraphs in Simpson, W.K. (ed.), *The literature of ancient Egypt. An Anthology of Stories, Instructions, Stelae, Autobiographies, and Poetry*, 3rd ed., New Haven and London 2003, p. 81, with n. 1; cf. Wente, E.F., 'The Egyptian Conjunctive as a Past Continuative', *JNES* 21 (1962), pp. 304-311 (see p. 309).

Some of these phrases are time expressions, as in the examples just given, or in

> *s(s)w sbq nꜣ i-ir ḫpr*
> 'Few days that happened, ...' or 'Soon after, ...'.[7]

At *Egyptians and Amazons* 2/29, for example, this phrase follows the call to arms made by the Queen of the Land of the Women, Sarpot, and indicates that her troops are quick to assemble from all parts of her country, and so the plot can move forward immediately. Another common time expression is

> *tꜣ wnw.t n nwe r-ir Pr-ꜥꜣ r pꜣ wr ꜣbṯ Pꜣ-qll irm Pꜣ-mi irm pꜣy=w mšꜥ*
> 'The moment that Pharaoh saw the Chief of the East Peklul and Pami and their forces, ...'.[8]

Here the king is dismayed to be confronted, immediately upon their arrival at his court in Tanis, by the Egyptian heroes who are the most contemptuous of his rule and conduct, and a belligerent dialogue follows.

All the examples cited so far refer to moments or passages of time—a very natural way to signpost the progress of a story, especially as Demotic narratives normally follow a very straightforward chronological sequence, often entirely linear. However, structural signposts also take other forms, and time expressions are not especially privileged in this role. There are perhaps two other groups of key phrases especially worthy of recognition. One refers to movement. For example,

> *twnw -s pꜣ irpꜣy Pꜣ-di-Ḫnsw*
> 'The Prince Petechons arose, ...'.[9]

Here Petechons arms himself for a fresh day's fighting against Queen Sarpot, in spite of the fact that, on the previous day, the two were smitten by love for each other on the battlefield. The same phrase evidently introduces Sarpot's corresponding preparations for battle in the following damaged line. The phrase is standard in the Inaros-Petubastis texts whenever a warrior prepares to fight.

Another example is

> *ꜣlꜥ nꜣ rmṯ.w ꜥꜣy r mr ir=w skl šꜥ pḥ.ṱ r Ḏꜥny*
> 'The notables went up on board and they sailed until reaching Tanis, ...'.[10]

This passage stands between a dialogue, in which the heroes Petechons and Pami stir each other to action, and their confrontation with the king (the same confrontation cited above). It might, very reasonably, be seen as a straightforward and natural account of what happened.[11] However, a shift of scene such as this is routinely marked (with minor differences in phraseology) by the sequence *going on board—sailing* (or *not tarrying*)*—arriving*. This degree of standardisation is far from inevitable.

---

[7] For example, *Egyptians and Amazons* 2/29, 8/32 (Hoffmann, *Ägypter und Amazonen*); cf. P. Rylands 9, 2/5, 21/5, and the discussion in Vittmann, G., *Der demotische Papyrus Rylands 9* (Ägypten und Altes Testament 38), 2 vols, Wiesbaden 1998, v. 2, p. 317.

[8] P. Krall 8/23-24 (Hoffmann, *Der Kampf*).

[9] *Egyptians and Amazons* 5/3.

[10] P. Krall 8/22-23.

[11] It may be worth specifying for non-specialist readers that in ancient Egypt travel up and down the Nile Valley would naturally be *by river*.

A third group of key phrases includes a reference to an emotion, or rather a display of emotion. A word used frequently is *tḥ*(*r*), 'to become troubled' (there is room for debate on the etymology of this word or words[12] but the issue need not be pursued here). For example

> *tḥr ḥꜣt pꜣ rpꜥy Pꜣ-di͗-Ḫnsw r-ḏbꜣ [nꜣy=s md.t.w] ḏd*
> 'The mind of the Prince Petechons became troubled because of [her words], saying...'.[13]

Petechons is dismayed that his new ally and lover Queen Sarpot is glad at the withdrawal of their Indian enemy, and that she seems to lack a proper warrior's commitment to all-out war; a dialogue between them then follows, in which their views and plans are set out vigorously.

A word that may perhaps be ranked with the emotions is *sby*, 'to laugh', or 'to smile' or 'to grin'. This naturally occurs as an action (that is, as a past narrative verb) rather than expressing an emotional state. For example

> *sby Nꜣ-nfr-kꜣ-Ptḥ ḏd*
> 'Naneferkaptah laughed, saying...'.[14]

Here Ahwere is delighted and relieved that Setna has come back to return the magical book of Thoth, but her husband Naneferkaptah has always known that Setna would have no option but to restore the book to them, and the phrase signposts that he is about to show superior knowledge.

Another action, already mentioned, that involves an emotion, is

> *bn-pw=f gm mꜣꜥ (nb) n pꜣ tꜣ i͗w=f n-i͗m=f*
> 'He did not know (literally, find) where on earth he was', that is, 'He was amazed', 'shocked', or 'obsessed, infatuated'.[15]

Instances of this expression normally warn the audience that the character who is amazed will quickly react in a fashion that will propel the story forward.

An example where the sense is entirely transparent is at the moment when Petechons and Queen Sarpot first fall in love on the battlefield, and each, in turn, 'did not know a place on earth where she/he was'.[16]

Alarm is expressed when a character utters a loud cry. For example, in P. Spiegelberg Pharaoh twice (in what is preserved) gives way to his surprise and dismay at fresh calamities:

> *wn Pr-ꜥꜣ rꜣ=f (r pꜣ i͗tn) n sgp ꜥꜣ i͗w=f ḏd*
> 'Pharaoh opened his mouth (to the ground) in a great cry, saying...'.[17]

A special case is when the phantom seductress Tabubu in *First Setna* abruptly terminates Setna's sexual advances with a cry, and Setna is rudely awakened from what seems to have been a kind of nightmare.[18] In *Second Setna* 2/14, the same idiom is used, not as a key structural phrase, but of the agonised scream of the rich man undergoing torture in Amente, in the

---

[12] See Erichsen, W., *Demotisches Glossar*, Kopenhagen 1954, p. 653.1, Westendorf, W., *Koptisches Handwörterbuch*, Heidelberg 1965-1977, p. 257, Černý, J., *Coptic Etymological Dictionary*, Cambridge 1976, p. 203, and Vycichl, W., *Dictionnaire étymologique de la langue copte*, Leuven 1983, p. 226.

[13] *Egyptians and Amazons* A 2/x+20.

[14] *First Setna* 5/39-6/2 (sic).

[15] For example *First Setna* 3/20, 5/1.

[16] *Egyptians and Amazons* 4/26, 27.

[17] P. Spiegelberg 5/16-17; 9/11.

[18] *First Setna* 5/29-30.

afterlife.[19] Fear, as opposed to alarm, is not an emotion that belongs here. This is partly because the Egyptian root *snḏ*,[20] Demotic *snt*,[21] primarily serves to indicate the power of instilling fear, rather than the emotion felt by those affected. This can be seen in the closing sentence from a letter sent to try to persuade the warrior hero Petechons to come to the aid of the king's supporters at Thebes:

> *my ỉr-rḫ pꜣ mšꜥ n Kmy n tꜣy=k snte ỉrm pꜣy=k nhr*
> 'May the people of Egypt know your fearsomeness and your terrifyingness',[22]

and perhaps in

> *r-wn wꜥt snty* [ꜥꜣ].*t ḫpr n pꜣ lms n rn=f*
> 'while there was a [great] fearsomeness in this *rms*-boat'[23]

—neither of which, plainly, is acting as a key structural phrase of the kind under discussion here. The second example simply closes and sums up an elaborate description of the impressive 'flagship' that has arrived, leading a fleet bearing fresh opponents of the family of Inaros.

Anger

Expressions for an outburst of anger may be set alongside these phrases. These are all actions, not expressions for a state of mind. The vocabulary is consistent. The basic word is *ḫ̂ꜥr*, 'to become angry'.[24] For example

> *tꜣ wnw.t ḏd nꜣy r-ỉr=f ḫ̂ꜥr ꜥnḫ-Ḥr sꜣ-nsw m-qty pꜣ ym*
> 'The moment that he said these things, ꜥAnkh-Hor the King's Son became angry like the sea, ...'.[25]

ꜥAnkh-Hor here is reacting to an increasingly confrontational dialogue between himself and his rival, the 'young priest': he then immediately arms himself for combat. Similarly, later in the same text, the same phraseology is applied to a different character:

> *ḫ̂ꜥr=f m-qty pꜣ ym*
> 'He became angry like the sea'.[26]

---

[19] Key phrases including a 'great cry' do occur in *Second Setna*, for example at 5/2-3 and 6/19.
[20] *Wb.* iv.182.2ff.
[21] Erichsen, *Demotisches Glossar*, p. 440.1.
[22] P. Spiegelberg 13/6-7; Petechons' furious reaction to the letter is discussed below. A similar phrase is used of the lion at *Myth of the Sun's Eye* 17/10-11: 'The beasts of the desert knew his fearsomeness and his terrifyingness'.
[23] P. Krall 14/10-11.
[24] Erichsen, *Demotisches Glossar*, p. 351.5; *Chicago Demotic Dictionary* s.v. The orthography varies, partly because of dialect differences.
[25] P. Spiegelberg 3/15-16 (Spiegelberg, W., *Der Sagenkreis des Königs Petubastis nach dem Strassburger demotischen Papyrus sowie den Wiener und Pariser Bruckstücken*, Leipzig 1910). The passage continues '...and his gaze was a burning flame, and his mind turned to dust like the eastern desert, and he said...' (3/16-18).
[26] P. Spiegelberg 13/12-13. The passage in full is 'The letter–it was folded, and sealed with the signet of the Chief of the East Paklul. It was handed to Hakoris, and he travelled northwards by night as by day. After a little while, he reached Per-Sepet. He did not delay going to the place where the Prince Petechons was. He gave him the letter. He read it, and he understood every word that was written upon it. He became angry like the sea, and stormed (*ỉr=f gsm*) like a furnace, and he said...' (7-14).

Here Petechons explodes with resentment against the king, but determines that he and Pami will indeed become involved in the escalating conflict at Thebes, at least in support of their own kinsmen—a crucial turning point in the story.

A special instance of interspersed outbursts of rage is found in the *Myth of the Sun's Eye* text.[27] The overarching story is of the god Thoth, in the form of a little 'monkey-wolf', trying to persuade the fearsome goddess Tefnut, Eye of Raʿ, in the form of an 'Ethiopian cat', to return calmly to Egypt. The text is punctuated by the Ethiopian cat's reactions to Thoth's attempts to placate her: her displays either of anger or of joy and contentment, which both frame and trigger the episodes—the embedded fables—that are the main business of the text:

> The moment that the Ethiopian cat heard the words, she laughed (*s3by=s*) again.... (4/2)
> She spoke with him—that is, the Ethiopian cat, and her mind was ablaze, her lips were on fire.... (8/10)
> The little monkey-wolf saw that the Ethiopian cat's mind was disturbed (*tẖr*): her face was dark, she was standing to her claws (i.e. tensed?), and her gaze was cast down to the ground.... (9/29-30)
> She laughed (*s3by=s*)—that is, the Ethiopian cat, and her mind was joyful at the words that the little monkey-wolf had said.... (15/28-29)

The root *ḫʿr* itself *is* used in the text, but not in these key phrases—except, as a noun, to indicate quite the reverse of becoming angry:

> *t3 nṯr.t lk=s n p3y=s ḫ̂ʿr*
> 'The goddess—she ceased from her anger'.[28]

Earlier Anger

Turning, more briefly, to earlier texts, outbursts of anger, alongside other emotions, may be found in Egyptian royal inscriptions. For example, the following occur in the Gebel Barkal inscription, or Victory Stela, of King Piye (mid-eighth century BCE):

> Then [His Majesty] heard [this] defiantly, laughing and amused.... (5-6)
> Then His Majesty raged because of it like a panther.... (23)
> Then His Majesty burst forth to revile his army, raging at it like a panther.... (30-1)
> Then His Majesty raged against it like a panther, saying.... (92)[29]

After expressing his anger,[30] on each occasion the king then proceeds to show his royal decisiveness and authority by announcing his plans or issuing orders. The phrases therefore are an integral part of the inscription's presentation of the king within the genre of the *Königsnovelle*.[31] They contrast with phrases rounding off an episode by expressing the king's satisfaction:

[27] De Cenival, F. *Le Mythe de l'Oeil du Soleil. Translittération et traduction avec commentaire philologique* (Demotische Studien 9), Sommerhausen 1988.
[28] *Myth of the Sun's Eye* 13/19.
[29] The translations are those of Robert Ritner in Simpson, *Literature of Ancient Egypt*, pp. 367-385; cf. the text-edition by Grimal, N.-C., *La stèle triomphale de Pi(ʿankh)y au Musée du Caire*, Le Caire 1981.
[30] The word that Ritner translates as 'raged' is the same word for anger that is standard in the Demotic stories, *ḫʿr*.
[31] Loprieno, A., 'The "King's Novel"', in Loprieno, A., (ed.), *Ancient Egyptian Literature. History and forms* (Probleme der Ägyptologie 10), Leiden 1996, pp. 277-295, and Hofmann, B., *Die Königsnovelle. 'Strukturanalyse am Einzelwerk'*, Wiesbaden 2004.

Then His Majesty was satisfied at it.... (144)
His Majesty then sailed southward, with his heart gladdened.... (154-5)[32]

In New Kingdom narratives[33] bursts of anger occur in much the same general manner as in the Demotic stories, although in very variable quantity.[34] For example, in the *Two Brothers*, once each the brothers become 'like an Upper Egyptian leopard (in anger)' (3/8, 5/5), and elsewhere there are other suggestions of anger but in quite different phraseology. The Prince of Naharin in the *Doomed Prince* 'became very greatly angry' (6/9-10) at the news that his daughter wished to marry a worthless refugee from Egypt—which is how the Prince had chosen to present himself. The rather frequent bursts of anger from several deities—but especially Raᶜ and Seth—in the *Contendings of Horus and Seth* have been discussed in detail by Sweeney.[35] In *Wenamun*, the Prince of Byblos is angry with Wenamun for having arrived without proper documents (1/53), and with his own courtier for addressing a remark (obscure to us, but evidently out of order) to Wenamun (2/46). These two public displays of anger perhaps contribute to a portrait of the Prince as an authoritative—king-like—figure.

In earlier narratives, strikingly, anger is more often implied than directly mentioned. For example, the *Westcar* papyrus[36] mentions that characters are pleased or sad, but not angry. In one of the stories-within-a-story, the magician Webaoner is informed that his wife is conducting an affair during his absences from home. It would seem natural for him to feel emotion on discovering his wife's adultery, but the narrative merely recounts his efficient revenge, which, at the end of the episode, meets with the king's approval. Remarkably, there is no phraseology relating to anger in the Middle Kingdom's most substantial story, and one which enjoyed a long reception, *Sinuhe*.[37]

Conclusions

The material has been presented very selectively here, but some conclusions may yet be offered.

The stories that concern themselves with anger, and that use key phrases involving anger as structural signposts in the narration, refer to public outbursts or displays of anger, intended to make an impression: quite the opposite of smouldering, concealed resentment. Anger is not so much an emotion as an expression or demonstration of emotion, in parallel with sadness or joy or laughter; it is not an illness or a state of possession. The principal characters who can indulge in such displays are the king and, naturally, deities. When, as cited above, the warrior Petechons in P. Spiegelberg became 'angry like the sea', he perhaps was arrogating to himself the royal privilege of anger, precisely because he did not accept King Petubastis's right to rule, and made no secret of his contempt.[38]

---

[32] Translations: Ritner in Simpson, *Literature of Ancient Egypt*.
[33] Translations of the best preserved texts may conveniently be found in Lichtheim, M., *Ancient Egyptian Literature. A book of readings*, v. 2: The New Kingdom, Berkeley 1976, pp. 195-230, or Simpson, *Literature of Ancient Egypt*, pp. 67-124, and the standard text-editions are in Gardiner, A.H., *Late-Egyptian Stories*, Bruxelles 1931-1932.
[34] The vocabulary is different: the root used is *qnd* or *ḥḏn*.
[35] Sweeney, *JEA* 88.
[36] Translations: Lichtheim, M., *Ancient Egyptian Literature. A book of readings*, v. 1: The Old and Middle Kingdoms, Berkeley 1973, pp. 215-222, or Simpson, *Literature of Ancient Egypt*, pp. 13-24.
[37] Translations: Lichtheim, *Ancient Egyptian Literature*, v. 1, pp. 222-235, or Simpson, *Literature of Ancient Egypt*, pp. 54-66.
[38] Explicitly at P. Spiegelberg 13.15. Of course, ᶜAnkh-Hor, the King's Son, also indulges in anger in P. Spiegelberg 3/15-18, as quoted above, but he is in a special position as son of King Petubastis, who is portrayed precisely as himself lacking in decisiveness and authority.

The point is not that an outburst of anger in itself intimidates those at whom it is directed. Indeed, in the texts, the reaction of the bystanders is of no account. Rather, it sets out a claim to power. In its context in a narrative, it is a spark of ignition for agency. A display of anger is followed by decisions, by commands, by action. The Egyptian wisdom literature (the phraseology of which has not been our concern here) in general presents indulgence in a fit of temper as something to be avoided, as it is an imprudent strategy for gaining worldly success; rather one must expect anger from a superior, and learn to cope with it. So, ordinary mortals can achieve little by displaying anger in an attempt to get their own way.[39] An Egyptian king, however, whether in narratives or in the discourse of royal inscriptions, may employ anger as an aspect of his agency—his authority and his power to get things done—because that is what society expects of him.

[39] Mark Collier points out to me that this might be in keeping with the seeming reluctance to express anger directly in Egyptian letters of the late New Kingdom.

Time and Space in Ancient Egypt

The importance of the creation of abstraction

David A. Warburton

Introduction

Man exists in time and space: we are constrained by these limits—if by no others. Only the written word or an artistic creation can permit a mortal to overcome these limits. Yet this victory is pyrrhic: language, art and architecture are means by which humans achieve immortality, yet the constraints demand that even immortality achieved by these means remains restricted to the limits of the horizon of mankind.

It is thus highly significant that—although we are biologically far older—our understanding of the human past abruptly changes as we cross the threshold of the invention of writing. The invention of writing accompanied the creation of urbanism and political structures. Like writing, monumental public architecture and complex art are also among the innovations of this age which are still with us, for material culture was also transformed with the appearance of the states.

Yet the written sources are assigned an almost unique role when approaching ancient thought. By contrast, one can argue—as is our intention here—that art and architecture contributed significantly to the development of conceptual thought. Following this argument means that meaning can be recognized in non-verbal forms of expression; it would also signal a cognitive change which is not ancient and biological, but recent and historical.

Regardless of perception, existence takes place in time and space, yet the perception of time and space is decisive for any understanding of being. We argue that Ancient Egypt played a dual role by creating means of expressing time and space which ultimately changed perception. Understanding this means throwing our understanding of "meaning" as expressed through verbal expression into doubt, and examining the means exploited by the Egyptians.

For several millennia after the dawn of history, the most widely recognized form of expression was verbal. With the appearance of cinema, television and advertising the image is recovering its value as means of conveying information. However, the image was never entirely discarded: from ancient murals to medieval illustrated manuscripts, imagery featured as a means of expression. Furthermore, architecture continued to play a role from before the beginning of history through to the present day.

Thus, although we tend to neglect them, assuming that "meaning" is to be sought in verbal expression actually precludes access to important avenues which give access to a culture which exploits other means. Egyptian understanding of time and space was more human influenced than ours.

Of particular interest to us here is an observation Groenewegen-Frankfort made when surveying the art forms of the Ancient Near East and the Bronze Age Mediterranean:

> In trying to penetrate ... what might—for lack of a better word—be called the implicit meaning in [artistic representations of] scenes, I found that the unexpected happened: both significance and formal peculiarities proved strictly correlated as soon as they were

seen under the aspect of their space-time implications. In fact changes in the one corresponded most strikingly with changes in the other, and spatial idiosyncracies therefore suddenly became 'significant'.[1]

She also stressed that there was a significant development at the beginning of the historical period in which "significant spaces" were created in art in a fashion which contrasted substantially with Palaeolithic art. Thus, mere representation and art are not simply alternative means of communication, but actually change at the same time that writing developed in the urban Near East. One of the most important changes concerns the development of an understanding of space.

Although Groenewegen-Frankfort consciously distanced herself from Krahmer,[2] we will argue that some of Groenewegen's observations about space can be incorporated into a system encompassing Krahmer's understanding of the static space of Egyptian art. And that this has significant philosophical implications not only for our understanding of Egyptian conceptions of space, but also of history.

We thus cover several different points. The central point is the degree to which ancient Egypt contributed to the human capacity to achieve an understanding of being. We argue that the invention and development of social institutions and public architecture contributed to a transformation of the human mind, and that writing is merely one of several decisive phenomena. Yet writing alone had substantial repercussions in academic discussions: almost eclipsing these other forms of expression.

The subsidiary points relate to the nature of "being" in ancient Egypt as expressed in art and language, where we perceive a clash in the different theoretical approaches which have dominated the study of Egyptian art.

At the centre is the issue of "understanding", grasped in terms of recognizing and expressing a "meaning". Thus, perception, expression, and content are the central issues related to "meaning". Today, it is assumed that meaning exists independent of time and space and language—in this perception, the popular and scholarly concept of finding "meaning" is the basis of human existence. Under this conception, it is assumed that meaning exists independently of humans, i.e., that it is "found".

Under the pressure of cognitive advances, human existence is increasingly understood as being biological and physical, rather than historical and conceptual. If one were to follow this latter line of reasoning to its logical end, one would find that the human adventure is not so much about the "discovery" of "meaning", but rather the creation or production of meaning: "meaning" is "invention" not "discovery". But nevertheless a process which is intrinsically biologically human, a part of our existence. We argue that this is entirely possible, but stress that significant steps in the process may not have taken place as a result of evolutionary neurological changes in the Pleistocene, but are rather historical artefacts created as a result of developments during the Bronze Age. In this sense, the biological argument about human nature is linked to cultural history, with the biological framework merely a platform upon which cultural activity erected a superstructure in recent times. We argue that one of the keys to understanding this can be found in the sources of Ancient Egypt.

One of the peculiarities of ancient Egypt is that many of the thoughts associated with that civilization are viewed as abstract, spiritual and timeless, whereas the forms of expression chosen by the Egyptians—both in art and language—were highly concrete. We argue that this is a crucial key to understanding developments, yet one that is generally overlooked—precisely

[1] Groenewegen-Frankfort, H.A., *Arrest and Movement: An Essay on Space and Time in the Representational Art of the Ancient Near East*, London 1951, pp. xxiii-xxiv.

[2] Krahmer, G., *Figur und Raum in der Ägyptischen und Griechisch-Archaischen Kunst* (=Hallesches Winkelmannsprogramm 28), Halle 1931

because we reduce meaning to linguistic expressions, and thus obscure developments rather than highlighting them.

It is in this sense that we stress the specifically concrete nature of Egyptian expression, and the absence of abstraction. Frustration with the incapacity of words to express thought might appear to be a constant of philosophical development, and in this sense one could suggest that the expression of Egyptian thought did not differ from our own when facing obstacles. However, there is a vast difference between the vocabularies available to a Nietzsche or a Foucault as opposed to a Ptahhotep.

In Junge's analysis of Ptahhotep, *jb* "the heart", is rendered as *Herz,* but also as *Geist, Sinnesart, Gesinnung, Seele, Gemüt* and *Vernunft.*[3] Obviously, this is one way of representing Egyptian thought to the modern reader. However, it is equally obvious that three thousand years of development have expanded the vocabulary available. Furthermore, it is not clear that the abstract concepts which Junge projects into Ptahhotep actually correspond to what was in the Egyptian "mind" (for which there is no word–except *jb*). Obviously, Junge is correct in assuming that the concepts did develop, and that they must have had an origin–and that this origin cannot be far from Ptahhotep's time. However, it is not clear that these thoughts were already in the Egyptian mind.

It is apparently difficult to understand the degree to which we should be cautious about projecting abstraction into Egyptian thought, simply because we are accustomed to assume that verbal abstraction is normal–and that it is the only form of abstraction. In our world, words and images serve a purpose in conveying a message, and our world has thus inherited the basic concept of concrete images from Egypt, but it has also transformed the concrete messages into abstract forms, expressed verbally.

The scene in *Book of the Dead* Spell 125 shows the heart itself being weighed on a real scale against the feather of Maat. Anubis, one of the gods of the necropolis and the dead is shown verifying the measurements, and Thoth, the god of the bureaucratic class records the results. We refer to this as a judgement scene, but it is actually a mere matter of verification. The iconography is obviously culturally conditioned, but one needs no real introduction in order to understand it, if one understands some Egyptian.

In western iconography, the pans of the scale of Justice are empty and the goddess of Justice is responsible for prosecution, verification and execution. Yet she is blindfolded so that she could not verify if she wanted to, and under the circumstances using her sword usefully is out of the question.

Obviously, the metaphor at the heart of our western image of Justice came from Egypt, but in the Western version the message and its form have changed substantially. Each element has acquired an allegorical meaning, which can be verbally interpreted. As we understand the symbol, we do not register the incongruities in the message as it is transmitted in our societies: it is completely overshadowed by the understanding of the abstract concept of Justice. This western image can be dissected and interpreted, both historically and metaphorically–and indeed it must be for it is incomprehensible.

Although similar, the Egyptian version was quite different. Maat was the weight which automatically meant that the scales tilted; Anubis and Thoth could simply observe the results. The heart itself was being measured. Thus there is much less content to be interpreted than in the Western scene. There is no question of abstract meanings.

The usual method as applied in modern Western critical analysis is that typified by Panofsky in *Meaning in the Visual Arts,* where he traces images and allegorical expressions in the works of Dürer (and colleagues) back through the Middle Ages, Classical Greece, and finally (on occasion) to ancient Egypt. By the Middle Ages and the Renaissance, such images had become laden with meaning, and Panofsky could dissect the layers. However, once he had

---

[3] Junge, F., *Die Lehre Ptahhoteps und die Tugenden der ägyptischen Welt* (=OBO 193), Fribourg 2003. Cf. Warburton, D., Review of Junge, *Ptahhotep, Discussions in Egyptology* 59 (2004), p. 99.

arrived in Egypt, Panofsky could not offer any such metaphorical interpretation. The Egyptian images had a significance which was immediate and clear: there were no hidden messages. The concept of abstraction was foreign to their art and language, and thus we argue that the Egyptian use of such images was utterly different from that of Western art—yet the Western images can be traced back to the Egyptian.

We argue that these concepts were brought into existence, and in recent times as a result of exchanges between societies (as in this case). Thus the heart has disappeared from the Western version of the scales of Justice, who is a specific deity with her own symbols (woman in classical garb, scales, blindfold, sword) which each require interpretation. The current writer stresses that this is part of our form of abstraction which no longer depends upon the images or the concrete elements. The verbal expression of the meaning takes precedence and the image is just a way of expressing the verbal thought. And this verbal expression has many nuances, as revealed in Junge's translations of *jb*. These concepts are distinct in our world.

To deny that the Egyptians felt differently would be absurd, as the language and the imagery confirm their way of thinking and testify to their way of expression. Our object here is to examine this, arguing that the Egyptians encoded complex thought in material form which they did not necessarily express in language. And also that they did not necessarily assign linguistic forms of expression to what we call abstraction. In fact there are additional "messages" in their art which cannot be recovered by the conventional methods of the interpretation of art, i.e., looking for a verbally expressed metaphorical meaning.

Responses to these forms of expression vary, but in general, the current writer has the impression that scholarly approaches suggest an effort to search for expressions of thought and meaning in forms familiar to us, most of them based on the assumption of a fundamentally human thought structure and the paramount use of language in expressing meaning. In this vision, "meaning" as expressed in language is immanent and inherent, and the difficulty is that of recognizing the means by which "meaning" comes to be expressed.

By contrast, the author contends that the means by which meaning came to play this role are historical and cognitive rather than biological and neural.[4] Our point of departure in the following will thus deal simultaneously with theoretical approaches and forms of expression.

Cognition, Language, Art, and Architecture

The Egyptians integrated the imagery and architecture of an urban civilization into their writing system. When viewing these phenomena in order to grasp the underlying system of classification, Goldwasser observed the following:

> Theories addressing the question of how knowledge is organized usually draw on evidence obtained from three principal sources: linguistic data acquired from local informants in non-literate societies, psychological experiments, and the study of diachronic and synchronic linguistic data in literate societies.[5]

While this is true, it does not necessarily mean that this is the correct fashion of approaching one of those civilizations which actually gave rise to the foundations of the linguistic means of classifying information. Our concern here is to approach the physical objects with the argument

[4] For reasons which cannot be elaborated here, the author is convinced that "meaning" is a variable dependent upon human society, and that Egypt played a crucial role in creating this state of affairs. This has substantial implications for our understanding of human perception and expression. Paradoxically, in order to explore the implications of this assumption in the context of Ancient Egypt, it is not necessary to agree with the fundamental assumption.

[5] Goldwasser, O., *Prophets, Lovers, and Giraffes* (=GOF IV 38/3), Wiesbaden 2002, p. 2.

that artefacts also contain information about systems of classification. Baines has defined this alternative quite clearly:

> Art served the ordered cosmos... It defined, encapsulated and perpetuated that cosmos.[6]

Our goal here is not to explore the superficial aspects of the artistic production of Egypt, but rather the implications of the underlying principles in terms of our understanding of Egyptian thought. Our approach differs from that of Kemp & Rose, but they correctly observed that in ancient Egypt,

> the Golden Section proportion ... was never recognized as such, and thus was not coded... The fluidity with which different factors mixed was aided by the way that the Egyptians moved from concept to actuality. ... [The procedure itself] is important for it reveals a mode of thinking and a process of ad hoc working that has grown unfamiliar to the modern Western and Western-influenced world.[7]

We will argue that far more than mere subconscious concepts determined the creation of Egyptian art, and that these betray thought processes complementary with a non-verbally expressed system of spatial-temporal classification. The "Western and Western-influenced" systems of thought referred to by Kemp & Rose were among the means by which verbally expressed thought eclipsed evidence of other kinds of thought.

Before approaching this method, we must refer to the corollary of Goldwasser's assumption, as expressed by the Assyriologist Bottéro who remarked of objects that their "testimony is reticent, vague, ambiguous if not fallacious", concluding that "archaeological sources do not inform so much as illustrate what we know from elsewhere" (meaning from philological sources).[8]

In fact, however, it is difficult to claim that the philological sources really provide a substantial contrast to what Bottéro claims to be the fundamental weakness of archaeological sources. In the case of Spell 17 of the *Book of the Dead,* Rößler-Köhler has demonstrated that the spell was a compendium of incompatible and contradictory interpretations of the Beyond from the very beginning.[9] And Schenkel has argued that the commentaries in the predecessor text, Coffin Text Spell 335A, appear to be almost contemporary with the original intact text.[10] Thus, the capacity to translate the text and to interpret it does not lead to any clarity about its meaning, except to highlight the fact that the Egyptians had some vague and inconsistent ideas about the Netherworld–and that they were completely conscious of the problem.

And certainly, archaeologists could claim that one could reach essentially the same conclusions from archaeological material–without recourse to texts.[11] Thus, at the very minimum, one would be obliged to recognize that the texts do not offer clarity–and yet the claim of the verbally based school is that this is the way in which thought is expressed; and also the means by which thought can be approached, analyzed and understood. In fact, however, Assmann has stressed that it is impossible to arrive at a uniform interpretation of Egyptian

---

[6] Baines, J., 'On the Status and Purpose of Ancient Egyptian Art', *Cambridge Archaeological Journal* 4/1 (1994), p. 88.

[7] Kemp, B. and Rose, P., 'Proportionality in Mind and Space in Ancient Egypt', *Cambridge Archaeological Journal* 1/1 (1991), p. 127.

[8] Bottéro, J., *La Plus Veille Religion,* Paris 1998, pp. 59-60. (My translations throughout for works not in English, or not cited in translated versions).

[9] Rößler-Köhler, U., *Kapitel 17 des Ägyptischen Totenbuches* (=GOF IV, 10), Wiesbaden 1979, pp. 267-353.

[10] Schenkel, W., 'Zur Redaktions- und Überlieferungsgeschichte des Spruchs 335 A der Sargtexte', in Westendorf, W. (ed.), *Göttinger Totenbuchstudien. Beiträge zum 17. Kapitel* (=GOF IV, 3), Wiesbaden 1975, pp. 37-79.

[11] Warburton, D.A., 'Literature & Architecture - Political Discourse in Ancient Egypt', in Moers, G., Behlmer, H., Demuss, K. and Widmaier, K. (eds.), *jnt dr.w. Festschrift für Friedrich Junge,* Göttingen 2006, pp. 706-707.

understanding on the basis of a textual analysis of *Book of the Dead* Spell 17, and that one should not strive to.[12]

Evidently, philologists could claim knowledge of a considerable quantity of detail (in terms of myths, divine names, etc.), but there is no way that the contradictions and inconsistencies of this philological detail are not exactly as "vague", "ambiguous" and "fallacious" as Bottéro suggested was the weakness of archaeological evidence. Thus, one can state that the philological detail does not really have the advantages that Bottéro suggests. Even if the deities can be named, it is far from certain that we can actually grasp the "meaning".

Significantly, however, authors continue to approach the Egyptian religion with the concept of organizing and unifying the written sources into a uniform system—and yet it is clear from CT 335A that this uniform system never existed. For the author, the implication is that both Goldwasser and Bottéro are members of a dominant school simply claiming—but not demonstrating—that "meaning" can only be approached through language. Although Goldwasser has obviously relied heavily on the system of writing rather than forms of linguistic expression, we contend that writing is dependent on language, even if language is also heavily dependent upon writing. Sources from the world of "Art & Architecture" are really quite different, and these can be approached differently, whereas it is generally the case that when viewing art, scholars tend to assume that it can be reduced to a verbal meaning.

Furthermore, we argue that this fundamental assumption effectively dominates most archaeological and art historical work, as will be found in the works of Boardman,[13] Leroi-Gourhan,[14] Gombrich,[15] and Panofsky[16] (etc.). The underlying approach of this school is that any work of art reflects a previously conceived verbally expressed meaning. This way of viewing art reduces it to being an alternative means of expressing thoughts which were already expressed verbally.

However, the evidence is that verbally expressed thoughts are far from clear and coherent, as we noted above in Assmann's conclusion that BD 17 cannot be used to understand Egyptian religion. In fact, therefore, textual analysis has demonstrated that the basic premise of this school is an error. By contrast, archaeological analysis reveals that careful study can actually provide glimpses into systems of thought: thoughts which cannot be found in the texts.

Our concern here is specifically the importance of space and time, and here—despite his own observations—Assmann clearly shares this philological approach, assuming that meaning will be found by philological analysis.[17] By contrast, Hornung has demonstrated that the Egyptians used form, size, measurements, location and imagery to express thoughts which probably were not expressed in the form of a conscious verbal equivalent.[18] There can also be no doubt that both Krahmer[19] and Groenewegen-Frankfort[20] were persuaded that Egyptian art gave access to Egyptian understanding of space and time in a far more wide-ranging fashion than the specific cases for which Hornung has found evidence.

However, these approaches have never been systematized. When trying to develop a methodology for understanding art as a social institution, Gell dismissed the traditional, symbolic, understanding of art, and thus his work found little sympathy among those who assumed that a linguistic analysis should allow for such content.[21] Instead, one could argue that Gell was actually hitting at the most important, fundamental, role of art—as the key to

[12] Assmann, J., *Re und Amun* (=OBO 51), Fribourg 1983, p. 7 with note 8.
[13] Boardman, J. *The World of Ancient Art*, London, 2006.
[14] Leroi-Gourhan, A., *Les Religions des la Préhistoire*, Paris, 1964.
[15] Gombrich, E., *The Story of Art*, Oxford, 1972.
[16] Panofsky, E., *Meaning in the Visual Arts*, New York 1955.
[17] Assmann, J., *Zeit und Ewigkeit im Alten Ägypten* (=AHAW 1975/1), Heidelberg 1975.
[18] E.g., Hornung, E. *Valley of the Kings*, New York 1990, pp. 186-189.
[19] Krahmer, *Figur und Raum*.
[20] Groenewegen-Frankfort, *Arrest and Movement*.
[21] E.g., Coquet, M., Review of Gell, *Art and Agency*, in *L'Homme*, 157 (2001), http://lhomme.revues.org/document5658.html.

understanding social identity.[22] However, Cooney has recently demonstrated beyond the shadow of a doubt that the aesthetic aspects of Egyptian art must be considered when trying to estimate social value.[23] Rather than taking issue with these various approaches, we will merely assume that no one will contest the concept that Egyptian art played a fundamental role in the expression of Egyptian identity—and proceed to the next level.

Regardless of one's analysis of the meaning of any given work of art, we will assume that an original Egyptian creation will be immediately recognizable as such, just as an "Egyptianizing" piece will be eternally debatable. Obviously, each in their own way, such pieces express something fundamental which is not resolved by classifying the one as "Egyptian(?)" and other as "Levantine(?)". There are nuances which are lost to us, some of which may have been formulated in verbal thought and since lost—but also some elements which may never have been verbally expressed.

Our argument here is that thoughts may not have been expressed verbally until after the creation of the physical artefacts which inspired them, i.e. that thought requires stimulation (as is obviously the case with modern academic debate). Obviously, however, the creation of any work of art depends upon a complex mental interaction whereby compromises must be made in reducing time and space to a material expression. However, this mental process can also lead the artist to overcoming the constraints of time and space. This is accomplished by creating a work which endures on its own (e.g., a simple figurine), one which is copied, or indeed by creating a work which comes to represent an era (such as the pyramid of Cheops) or a world (such as the statues of Khafren).

Although we are accustomed to innovative original creations, most art in Antiquity was representative, and thus depended upon a capacity to reduce something to an essence which was then preserved in the form of the representation. Whether sculpture, relief or architecture, the procedure depended upon a process of mental transformation, whereby a real (or conceptual) thing was rendered concrete. Peculiarly, however, none of these processes involved requires verbal expression, as the entire process from conception & execution to exhibition & survival does not rely on verbal thought. And yet the key to the ultimate understanding of "meaning" as grasped by humans—that is, immortality—lies precisely in this process.

Creation of this type represents a capacity to express time and space in art without recourse to verbal expression. And analysis of this aspect can enable us to follow conceptual processes. We argue that the search for a superficial interpretation of the "meaning" of an object bears no relationship to the fundamental message which it conveys about world view. In fact, to some degree, this search is erroneous, as the medium imposes the problem of "meaning" on us. We understand this as perception, whereas the artist was working on the level of expression, and combining several different thoughts into a single creation. By definition, art is provocative and ambivalent and the idea that a meaning can be sought in the artwork itself may be mistaken. However, the fundamental and decisive cognitive processes which determined the creation of any given piece of art will betray the thoughts of the civilization—and in a fashion which is at once unequivocal, historical and not verbally expressed.

Virtually all complex art dates to the period after the invention of states and writing. Therefore it is arguably historical—and we would argue that it is erroneous to suggest that the basic thoughts as expressed in terms of perception and expression were present before the transformation of human society; and the absence of complex art represents a strong argument in this case. Thus, these societies gave birth to the context in which thought could leap to another level, rendering abstract thought, as we understand it, possible. Significantly, although neurologically possible, thought of this kind is not necessarily biologically innate. And, fundamental thoughts were not reproduced in writing or language. Understood thus, these thoughts provide access to a world view.

---

[22] Gell, A., *Art & Agency. An Anthropological Theory*, Oxford 1998.

[23] Cooney, K. M., *The Cost of Death*, (=EU 22), Leiden 2007, p. 6.

Time & Space in Art & Language

There are a number of Egyptian words which define time in a specific fashion (e.g., *ꜥḥꜥ*, *rnp.t*, *rk*, *hrw*, *sp*, *ꜣ.t*, *grḥ*, *tr*) and a few which define time more generally or conceptually (e.g., *nḥḥ*, *hꜣw*, *ḏ.t*). The same applies to space (e.g., *s.t*, *sp.t*, *njw.t*, *ẖꜣs.wt*, *tꜣ*, *tꜣš*). However, it has been pointed out that *ḏ.t* takes us into the time-space continuum, uniting solar cycles with geography. And Hornung has shown that this appears in art, in a fashion which is never expressed verbally:

> This extreme circumference of the existent, to which the Egyptians give the visual form of the "curled snake (*mḥn*)," is both spatial and temporal. The snake curled back on itself encompasses a four-dimensional world that has an end–which the spherical models of modern physics also present as turned back on itself; the Ouroboros seems to be the only visual symbol that shows this turning back on itself.[24].

This is a relatively simple and straight forward case of an artistic representation which expresses a thought which could be expressed verbally and is recognizable to us.

However, the principles underlying the creation of a work of art can be interpreted in the same fashion. When dealing with representations on taut surfaces (flat, cylindrical, globular), Groenewegen-Frankfort argued that the "relationship between two objects creates a significant void". This space creates a context for movement. At the same time, however, she also noted that

> ... For there is no way of transferring the contour of the human form, especially in movement, to a flat surface in which the problem of depth does not become acute.[25]

To skip forward, we will refer to one single example which must suffice for the understanding of the problem in ancient Egyptian art. Referring to the girl in the the tomb of Rekhmire, Groenewegen-Frankfort notes:

> In fact, when once and once only in the historical development of several millennia the three-quarter back view of a serving girl appears in a Theban tomb with the proportions of perfect functional rendering..., the effect is positively startling. She appears a strange disturbing phenomenon in a spatial world which, for better or worse, is alien to ours.[26]

In another reference to this same girl, she says

> In this otherwise smooth scene, however, the *trois quarts* back view of one of the girls ... is very startling indeed and seems quite incongruous; seen from a definite angle, she has–in contrast with all other figures–'corporeality', appears in fact in space. It is as if the artist was frightened by his own boldness, for he drew the feet adhering to the groundline in the traditional, and in this case absurd, old way.[27]

This approach represents the usual interpretation: Egyptian understanding of space was quite different from ours; Schäfer resolved the complexities by drawing on children's art.[28] However, a contemporary of Schäfer's took a very different line:

---

[24] Hornung, E., *Conceptions of God in Ancient Egypt*, Ithaca 1993, pp. 178-179.
[25] Groenewegen-Frankfort, *Arrest and Movement*, p. 6.
[26] Groenewegen-Frankfort, *Arrest and Movement*, p. 9.
[27] Groenewegen-Frankfort, *Arrest and Movement*, p. 93.
[28] Schäfer, H. *Principles of Egyptian Art*, Oxford 1986.

> In Egypt—where perspective was carefully observed as demonstrated by the occasional foreshortened figures—this could have led to the discovery of perspective as a form of artistic expression ... However these few attempts, which led nowhere and were thus consigned to oblivion, prove that this form of representation did not appeal to the Egyptians and that for them it was little more than a curiosity.[29]

The figurative ostraca from Deir el-Medineh make it certain that Krahmer's observation was correct, and that the failure to develop perspective was not a matter of a terror of the unknown, but rather a lack of interest. We argue that Krahmer was on the right track, and that we can usefully pursue the argument he began in the 1920's.

Krahmer's system was based on the assumption that the orthogonality of Egyptian art—both plastic and relief—must be understood in terms of a specific understanding of space. Krahmer compared our "Classical, perspective"-influenced understanding of space, which he termed "dynamic", with the "static space" of the Egyptians.[30] In his version, depth was effectively non-existent in Egyptian art, and one has the unnerving experience of noting that the Egyptians played with this lack of depth (as with the single shawl wrapped around three jackals, or the *ankh*-sign hanging off a mountain, both in TT 359).[31]

Rather than arguing that the Egyptians were "frightened" of perspective, we argue that we should be wary of imposing our understanding of time and space on them—and cautious in assuming that Egypt was merely a stage on the way to discovering the way "things should be done". Thus, rather than drawing back, we follow Krahmer.

Krahmer distinguishes a hypotactic (typically "Classical, perspective") form of art where each member of the human body is subordinated to the movement of the others, from the fundamentally different paratactic form (typically Egyptian) where each member is depicted as an ideal independent of others. For Krahmer, each of the systems must be understood in terms of dynamic and static space: hypotactic "Classical, perspective" art relies upon dynamic space; paratactic Egyptian art does not have depth: it understands the dimensions in what Krahmer terms "static space". Krahmer concludes:

> After these analyses it becomes completely clear that ... there is no difference between the "frontal view" in plastic and the "twisted view" of the reliefs, and that it is only because we conceive space as a dynamic unity that there appears to be a contrast... Depth plays a completely different role in Egyptian art, as indeed in all pre-perspective artistic conceptions.[32]

For Krahmer therefore, the cubic form which typifies so many Egyptian statues was not a cage within which the figure was imprisoned. Instead, each of the planes defining the sides, base, top and bottom of the statue were merely segments of the dimensions which continued infinitely in all directions, crossing each other perpendicularly. For Krahmer, the tension of the dimensions was the glue which held the various parts of Egyptian statues together. In fact, for Krahmer, a "three-dimensional" hypotactic Greek statue was not three-dimensional at all, but rather dimensionless; the Egyptian paratactic version was absolutely three dimensional in the sense that it came into existence where the dimensions met, and exploited the clash of the dimensions in static space to achieve perfection, in the balance between the dimensions.

---

[29] Krahmer, *Figur und Raum*, p. 64.

[30] The phrase "Classical, perspective" is a compromise here, used to designate those perspective styles appearing from the fifth-century onwards in Greece, and henceforth elsewhere. Neither "Greek" nor "Pre-Perspective" is adequate since obviously Archaic Greek art is still "Greek" and "pre-perspective" is a misnomer in light of the Egyptian evidence.

[31] E.g., Hodel-Hoenes, S., *Life and Death in Ancient Egypt*, Ithaca 2000, pp. 272-273.

[32] Krahmer, *Figur und Raum*, p. 65.

Krahmer's static space is thus explosive, rather than passive, like "Classical, perspective" space. This means that Egyptian space has a character which differs fundamentally from our own. When transferred from the art historical level to the philological and historical level, this understanding would imply that the concept of *ḏ.t* being a form of inert linear time or space must be abandoned. Including temporal depth—of which the Egyptians were fully conscious—among the dimensions of this kind would render Egyptian thought dynamic. Firstly, the linear character of time would be transformed. Secondly, the role of the human in creating history is also given priority. In this sense, the concept of the Egyptians having been conscious of the necessity of establishing and maintaining Maat becomes a question of the imposition of human will on the universe; history becomes a human endeavour.

The three dimensions visible in art take on a different importance; furthermore, they are combined with temporal depth to create a fourth dimension. This fourth dimension would be different from our own since depth and space would play a lesser role in the three dimensions of static space. It would mean including time as an integral part of the space-time continuum—which has hitherto eluded western science. Krahmer's view of art thus offers a comprehensive understanding of the Egyptian world view, but expressed in a fashion which is not visible in the texts or the language.

In spatial depth, however, there is one point where the Egyptian image of depth did not differ from our own. Groenewegen-Frankfort noted:

> Only the colour blue will, for obvious reasons, suggest pure depth.[33]

Thus, one can use a colour to depict spatial depth, and many of those who have seen it will have a vivid memory of the sky-blue background of the stele at the back of the tomb of Sirenput.[34] The light blue background of the stele gives it the impression of being a window—even though it is at the deepest part of a rock cut tomb. Obviously, we perceive depth here. This is important because: firstly, we noted that Krahmer's system basically assumed that the Egyptians did not assign spatial depth a crucial role, and secondly, because of a linguistic element, as expressed by Baines:

> ...blue plays no part in color symbolism in texts[35] (Baines 1985: 283)

Baines assumed that the Egyptian word *w3ḏ* covered green and blue, and that lapis lazuli, *ḫsbḏ*, was not an abstract colour term. Baines argued that ancient Egyptian corresponded to an early evolutionary stage of a model proposed by Berlin & Kay,[36] in which the Egyptian language had only four colour terms: black (*km*), white (*ḥḏ*), red (*dšr*) and green-blue (*w3ḏ*). It is evident that by dismissing *ḫsbḏ* and assigning *w3ḏ* to the green-blue spectrum Baines had denied that there was an Egyptian word for blue. Thus his observation about the absence of symbolic blue meanings in texts was not an observation or a conclusion but purely circular logic.

However, the Egyptian term *w3ḏ* was not green-blue, but actually green.[37] This means that the blue range was in fact unoccupied, and thus it is logical to adopt the stance of thoses scholars who have proposed that lapis lazuli occupied this part of the spectrum. Taking *ḫsbḏ* as a word for blue, Quirke argues that the theoretical structure upon which Baines relied was

[33] Groenewegen-Frankfort, *Arrest and Movement*, p. 5.

[34] Lange, K. & Hirmer, M. *Egypt*, London 1968, pl. XIII

[35] Baines, J., 'Color Terminology and Color Classification: Ancient Egyptian Color Terminology and Polychromy', *American Anthropologist* 87 (1985), p. 283.

[36] Berlin, B. and Kay, P., *Basic Color Terms: Their Universality and Evolution*, Berkeley 1969.

[37] Schenkel, W. 'Color terms in ancient Egyptian and Coptic', in MacLaury, R., Paramei, G. V., and Dedrick, D. (eds.), *Anthropology of Color: Interdisciplinary Multilevel Modeling*, Amsterdam, 2007, p. 226.

probably not applicable to Egyptian.[38] In fact, the use of lapis lazuli and blue pigments in Egyptian art and literature renders it impossible to maintain Baines's view.[39] Thus, blue must be recognized in the context of spatial and conceptual understanding–but a blue related to a specific material, and not an abstract blue.

This particular feature is of key importance for our argument since the scheme developed by Berlin & Kay recognized the Greek word for blue (*kyaneos*) and the Italian word for blue (*azzurro*) as "abstract colour terms" whereby both they and Baines denied that Egyptian *ḫsbḏ* could serve as an abstract word since it was concrete lapis lazuli (and the same treatment is proposed for the Akkadian word as well). However, like the French *azur* and the English *azure*, the Italian *azzurro* is derived from the Persian word for lapis lazuli (*lazuward*),[40] as the Greek is originally derived from the Akkadian word for the same stone (*uqnu*).[41] Thus, the words are not the product of an evolution in either of these languages, and they only became abstract when exported beyond the region where the material was common; only as loan words did they become abstract.[42]

Thus we can see that what later became abstract terms for colours were actually related to physical materials (as is indisputably the case for *ḥḏ*, "silver" / "white" in any case) in some languages and only by exchange did they become abstract. We argue that this did not really take place until the Iron Age or perhaps not even until the Middle Ages in Europe. It certainly does not seem to be present in the languages of the Bronze Age. At the same time, however, the use of blue in certain contexts in art, such as the tomb at Aswan, and the concept of the *sḫ.t mfk3.t*, the heavenly "field of turquoise", suggests that the Egyptians were fully conscious of the value of blue for expressing abstract spatial depth. Remarkable is that they were able to do this although (a) they had no word for blue, and although (b) their linguistic categories did not include an abstract word for space, and although (c) their artistic system did not rely on spatial rendering as we understand it.

Conclusions

Linear, static space is the context for historical activity, yet our historical horizon cannot reach beyond the invention of writing. Rather than appreciating this limit as applicable to human vanity, it has been assumed that it also applies to the understanding of meaning. The limits of verbal expression are thus imposed on meaning in a fashion which allows scholars to assume that meaning is invariably encoded in language. They contend that without written sources we lack access to meaning. This allows them to assume that complex thought was simply not recorded–rather than allowing that the urban civilisations of the Ancient Near East created the conditions which allowed it to come into existence.

In this discussion, we have tried to argue that the ancient Egyptian understanding of time and space was visible in their art, but not expressed in language; and also suggested that Egyptological approaches have obscured these processes.

We argue that social developments and art are generally disregarded in the analysis of thought, and understanding is assigned to language. At the same time, however–and this is our

[38] Quirke, S., 'Color Vocabularies in Ancient Egyptian', in Davies, W.V. (ed.), *Color and Painting in Ancient Egypt*, London, 2001, pp. 186-192

[39] For more detailed discussions, cf. Warburton, D. 'Basic color term evolution in light of ancient evidence from the Near East', in MacLaury, R., Paramei, G. V., and Dedrick, D. (eds.), *Anthropology of Color: Interdisciplinary Multilevel Modeling*, Amsterdam, 2007, pp. 229-246; Warburton, D., 'Colourful Meaning: Terminology, Abstraction, and the Near Eastern Bronze Age', in Johannsen, N., Jessen, M. & Jensen, H. J. (eds.), *Cross-sections through culture, cognition and materiality*, Aarhus, forthcoming.

[40] *Le nouveau Petit Robert de la langue française*, Paris 2007, p. 202.

[41] Von Soden, W., *Akkadisches Handwörterbuch*, Wiesbaden 1981, III: 1426.

[42] For this, see the literature in note 39, supra.

central argument—it is paradoxically assumed that this understanding can be projected back in time, and assigned to a biological paradigm, which extends back to before the dawn of history. The task of the archaeologist is merely to recognize the steps. Our argument here is that in this fashion, we can never appreciate the history of the creation of abstraction. Abstract space and thought are historical artefacts, and Egypt played a crucial role in creating them.

Therefore, our first point is that to understand the Egyptian system of classification, we must include their art and architecture, quite aside from their linguistic categories. Among features distinguishing Egyptian art and thought from Greek are:

Egypt	Greece
Artistic view as paratactic expression	Artistic view as perspective, hypotactic perception
Construction as extension	Construction as renewal
Space is explosive, static	Space as depth for dynamic human activity
Time is linear spatial, human future to be made in future	Time as human, but golden age in divine past

This system is not a mere system of classificatory distinctions: the distinctions allow insights into a foreign way of thought. There are differences in the art which betray contrasting means of temporal and spatial understanding.

But invisible here is the (far more important) fact that the verbal discourse of Ancient Greece also introduced the discussion of concepts which were never discussed in the Ancient Orient. Hitherto, it has been assumed that this reflected a weakness in pre-Greek thought. Now, however, the discovery of Babylonian mathematical sciences has opened the way to a science which was expressed in terms of results rather than discussion.[43] It has been alleged that Egyptian science was less advanced than the Babylonian, but Krauss's synthesis of the earliest Egyptian astronomical thought renders this impossible.[44] Significantly, these scientific thoughts were not expressed in the form of discourse.

In the same way, the complex thoughts visible in the artistic creations of Ancient Egypt were never expressed verbally: Greek practice represented an extraordinary leap in comparison to the methodology of the Ancient Near East. However, this means neither that the Egyptians did not cultivate such thoughts, nor that those expressed verbally by the Greeks are representative of ordinary forms of human thought which were merely unrecorded before the invention of writing.

Significantly, the Egyptians did "develop an interest in time and motion", although Kemp once suggested that they did not.[45] However, they approached the matter differently. The turquoise trees of chap. 17 of the *Book of the Dead* and the blue tree of TT 359 not only reveal that Egyptian trees were not invariably green (despite protests to the contrary, e.g., Wolf),[46] but also confirm that such exceptions give access to how the Egyptians did approach space (which is the precondition for approaching time and motion).

We must draw on Egyptian evidence to develop theoretical structures compatible with the results of recent scholarship, rather than trying to draw on existing theory and applying it to Ancient Egypt. This means approaching the material itself, both linguistic and architectural.

We contend that the Egyptian artistic forms were the essential precondition for the emergence of abstract verbal thought. Viewing Egyptian means of expression in art and

[43] Cf., e.g., Swerdlow, N. M., *The Babylonian Theory of the Planets*, Princeton, 1998.
[44] Krauss, R., *Astronomische Konzepte und Jenseitsvorstellungen in den Pyramidentexten*, Wiesbaden, 1997.
[45] Kemp, B. J., *Ancient Egypt*, London 1989[1], p. 4.
[46] Wolf, W., *Die Kunst Ägyptens*, Stuttgart, 1957, p. 68.

architecture from this standpoint means that we must abandon relying almost exclusively on the linguistic approach if we are really to understand Egyptian thought. Many linguistically expressed concepts, such as time and space, depend upon a foundation. We argue that these ideas depend upon a concrete form of expression in order for the linguistic form to appear. Thus, one cannot project the verbally known form of meaning back to an age before the creation of the art which made it possible for the conceptual systems to appear.

Defining the categories of what we seek means that we will find what we are looking for. To avoid confusion we must understand what happened in ancient Greece–but also what the Egyptians did. Only thus can we appreciate how the foundations for the transformation of human thought were established in Egypt.

Thus, we argue that by assuming abstraction as a condition and principle, we cannot find our concepts in Egypt–at least not without losing Egypt.

Abstract

Regardless of perception, existence takes place in time and space, yet the perception of time and space is decisive for any understanding of being. Ancient Egypt played a dual role by creating means of expressing time and space which ultimately changed perception. Understanding this means throwing our understanding of "meaning" as expressed through verbal expression into doubt, and examining the means exploited by the Egyptians. For several millennia after the dawn of history, the most widely recognized form of expression was verbal. With the appearance of cinema, television and advertising the image is recovering its value as means of conveying information. However, the image was never entirely discarded: from ancient murals to medieval illustrated manuscripts imagery featured as a means of expression. Furthermore, architecture continued to play a role from before the beginning of history through to the present day. Thus, although we tend to neglect them, assuming that "meaning" is to be sought in verbal expression actually precludes access to important avenues which give access to a culture which exploits other means. Egyptian understanding of time and space was more human influenced than ours.

Index of Egyptian and Greek words and expressions

Egyptian

Greek